# Assessment: A Practical Guide for Secondary Teachers

**Classmate Extra titles**

*Lesson Planning: Second Edition* – Graham Butt

*Managing Your Classroom: Second Edition* – Gererd Dixie

# Assessment: A Practical Guide for Secondary Teachers

**Howard Tanner and Sonia Jones**

continuum
LONDON • NEW YORK

**Continuum International Publishing Group**

The Tower Building
11 York Road
London
SE1 7NX

80 Maiden Lane
Suite 704
New York
NY 10038

*www.continuumbooks.com*

**British Library Cataloguing-in-Publication Data**
A catalogue record for this book is available from the British Library.

ISBN: 0-8264-8666-5 (paperback)

Typeset by Servis Filmsetting Limited, Manchester
Printed and bound in Great Britain by Antony Rowe Ltd, Chippenham, Wilts.

Assessment and Learning?
Mind the Gap!

# Contents

1 What do children need from assessment? 1
Introduction: What are our current assessment practices? 1
Why do we assess our students? 3
How can children learn from assessment 5

2 Formative assessment 19
What do we mean by formative assessment? 19
Informal formative assessment to support whole-class teaching 24
How can 'rich questioning' support informal assessment? 27
Formal versus informal target setting 34

3 Feedback and marking strategies 39
Planning for assessment in the short, medium and long term 39
What kind of feedback do students need? 46
Attitudes to assessment and learning 56

4 Self-assessment and learning to learn 59
Involving students in their own assessment 59
Developing peer-and self-assessment 65

5 Using examinations to support learning 80
High-stakes examinations versus formative assessment? 80
Teaching students to learn from summative assessment 88
The strategies for developing self-efficacy 91

# Contents

Metacognitive strategies: Review, refection and revision
    notebooks                                                    92
Preparation for examinations                      96
Post-examination review                             98
The impact of the DERS project                   99

6  Developing an effective learning culture: Strategies
    for change                                       101
Introducing formative assessment in your classroom    104
Developing a formative assessment culture in your
    department                                  112
Developing a formative assessment culture in your
    school                                        116
Revisiting Standards Comprehensive            119

*References*                                                   121

1

# What do children need from assessment?

## Introduction: What are our current assessment practices?

Let's begin by considering a school that we know quite well. Let's call it Standards Comprehensive. In this school, the teachers work very hard trying to provide interesting, challenging lessons; most of the students try to learn and are assessed frequently. In fact, assessing, recording and reporting are major features of school life in Standards Comprehensive. Teachers mark classwork, homework and tests on a regular basis and internal examinations are conducted every year. Baseline assessment information is collected and targets are set for students, classes and teachers. Records are maintained efficiently and in great detail. The effort and emotional energy put into assessment, recording and reporting by students and teachers is enormous.

And yet, in spite of all this effort, the results that the students of Standards Comprehensive gain in external examinations are unexceptional. In spite of exhortations from teachers, assessment events such as internal examinations and end-of-module tests do not seem to result in changes to students' learning behaviours or revision strategies. In fact, many of the lower attaining students seem almost resigned to their poor performance, accepting it as the natural order of things. Even the highest attaining students seem to take little notice of the errors they make in tests and examinations and gain little of value from the experience. Success often seems to be attributed to 'natural ability' or good luck; and failure to lack of natural ability or bad luck – either way there seems to be little to be done about it.

The assessment systems that are used in Standards Comprehensive don't even seem to support the teaching process very well. End-of-module tests and end-of-year examinations provide information about the success or failure of learning *after* the event, when it is too late for students or teachers to deal effectively with any misconceptions that are exposed. In any case, such tests and examinations are rarely analysed to identify difficulties with any degree of precision – there never seems to be enough time, and anyway the class will be handed on to a new teacher before those topics are taught again.

The information collected in Standards Comprehensive does not lend itself well to planning for learning and teaching. Its main uses are often:

- to create ability sets or bands;

- to provide information to parents on annual reports;

- to set long-term targets for teachers and students;

- to track progress towards external examinations.

However, a visitor from another planet would probably conclude that the main purpose of assessment in Standards Comprehensive School is to provide data for records to fill filing cabinets, or – in more advanced institutions – spreadsheets.

These criticisms of current common assessment practices are not new. For several years, a consistent message from Ofsted reports has been the 'indifferent quality of assessment compared with other aspects of teaching in secondary schools' (Ofsted 2003, p. 1). Poor assessment practices which fail to support learning and teaching to best effect seem to be remarkably resilient and resistant to change.

## Why do we assess our students?

There are many different end-users for assessment information but since the introduction of the National Curriculum, emphasis has been placed on audiences outside the classroom and uses associated with accountability and the management of the system. Although such managerial aims are valid in their own right, it is time to emphasize those functions of assessment which aim to improve the effectiveness of learning and teaching.

We group the aims of assessment under three broad headings: managerial, communicative, and pedagogical (Tanner and Jones 2003c, pp. 12–13).

*Managerial* aims for assessment include:

- demonstrating or testing the effectiveness of government policies;

- holding schools and LEAs accountable for students' progress;

- holding teachers accountable for the progress of their classes;

- motivating teachers through payment-by-results schemes such as the threshold;

- selecting students to benefit from a limited resource, e.g. university education;

- controlling the curriculum by emphasizing particular forms of knowledge such as Key Skills.

*Communicative* aims for assessment include:

- providing information to parents about their children's progress against nationally agreed standards;

- providing information to other teachers, educational institutions or employers about individual students' knowledge and skills;

- producing league tables of schools to inform parental choice;

- informing teachers and students which parts of the curriculum are considered valuable enough to examine.

*Pedagogical* aims for assessment include:

- evaluating the success of your own teaching;

- analysing students' learning and identifying misconceptions;

- supporting the teaching process by providing feedback to inform future planning;

- supporting the teaching process by identifying precisely what individuals and groups of students need to know to improve, in order to inform the planning of future teaching;

- giving students an appreciation of their achievements and encouraging success;

- motivating students and holding them accountable;

- supporting the learning process by helping students to identify areas of weakness or misunderstanding and suggesting strategies for development;

- encouraging students to develop skills of self-assessment;

- providing students with the information they require to become self-regulating learners.

Since the 1980s, the emphasis has been mainly on the managerial and communicative aims and, in particular, the need to sum up the extent to which children, teachers and schools have met particular standards. These functions of assessment are referred to as summative.

The pedagogical aims for assessment support the learning and teaching process. Such assessment is referred to as formative or, more recently, assessment *for* learning (AfL). Formative assessment has been demonstrated to exert a powerful influence on learning (Black and Wiliam 1998a, b) but, unfortunately, the emphasis placed on this function of assessment has been slight.

Assessment for learning may be defined as:

> The process of seeking and interpreting evidence for use by learners and their teachers to decide where the learners are in their learning, where they need to go, and how best to get there. (Assessment Reform Group 2002)

However, although AfL is strongly supported by the Qualifications and Curriculm Authority (QCA), its use remains limited:

> Systematic, rigorous and productive attention to the strengths and weaknesses of students' work remains the exception rather than the rule . . . In all subjects, feedback to students which helps them to improve is still too variable. (Ofsted 2004, p. 6)

## How can children learn from assessment?

Before we can begin to answer how children can learn from assessment, it is first necessary to consider how children learn. To most teachers and researchers it is obvious that the answer to this question is more complicated than just by being told! Although some low-level skills and facts may be learned through simple stimulus-response mechanisms, developed through mindless repetition, most useful knowledge requires more than this. To develop deeper knowledge, concepts and processes based on understanding, demands active, mindful and effortful participation by the learner.

Our view of learning is essentially socio-constructivist, in that we believe that in the end children must construct knowledge for themselves through their own efforts (Piaget 1977; Von Glasersfeld 1991). However, we do not think that the process of knowledge construction should take place in isolation, divorced from teaching and social interaction. Effective teachers orchestrate social conditions to encourage children to engage deeply with challenging tasks that demand the construction of new knowledge and concepts.

In order to learn, children must first become engaged with situations or tasks that are sufficiently challenging to demand the construction of new knowledge or new ways of looking at the world. Pitching lessons at a level that provides sufficient challenge without going 'over their heads' has always been an issue in lesson planning.

It has often been assumed that the ideal situation would be for the background knowledge of each child to be assessed accurately and then for an individualized learning programme to be devised based on their current knowledge. Many schemes of work developed in the 1970s and 1980s were based on this premise. Some recent computer software works on the same assumption. When the National Curriculum was introduced in 1988, its associated assessment and recording system was based on similar principles, and rapidly brought the system into disrepute amongst teachers for being overly bureaucratic and ignoring the social aspects of classroom life (Tanner 1992).

Assessment in the classroom will never be a precise science. What children can achieve depends on more than their individual cognitive abilities. Learning and academic performance depend on social and emotional factors as well as purely cognitive ones. What you can do depends on the context you are in, the friends you are with, the social expectations of the classroom or situation, and whether your emotional needs are being met, as well as your background knowledge and abilities. Children may even learn by thinking about the task being used for assessment! We like to use the photography metaphor, and consider every assessment to be a slightly blurred snapshot of a moving target that is often out of date before it can be developed or recorded!

Fortunately, it is a false premise that students can only learn when the task they are offered is at exactly the right level for their personal background, knowledge and experience. Whole-class teaching is able to proceed largely because children are actually able to learn when a task comes within *range* of their current knowledge – in the 'learning zone' (Newman *et al.* 1989). Effective teachers make continual, approximate assessments as teaching proceeds to keep the class in the learning zone. There is no need to record such continual assessments, because if they are effective, they should be out of date before the end of the lesson. The learning zone is based on what Vygotsky (1978, p. 86) called the 'Zone of Proximal Development' (ZPD).

> The zone of proximal development . . . is the distance between the actual developmental level as determined by independent problem solving and the level of potential development as determined through problem solving under adult guidance or in collaboration with more capable peers. (Vygotsky 1978, p. 86)

Three possible levels of difficulty for student tasks are shown in Table 1.1. At the lowest level, children are able to work unaided using only knowledge which is secure and well known. When

Table 1.1 The learning zone or ZPD (Tanner and Jones 2000b, p. 80)

| **Out of range** | | |
|---|---|---|
| Activities are too hard | Off-task behaviour | No learning |
| Work goes over their heads | Poor discipline | |
| **The learning zone or ZPD** | | |
| Activities can only be completed with help | Working noise Teacher kept busy | Maximum learning |
| **Current level** | | |
| Activities involve familiar and secure knowledge | Silent working Teacher not needed | No learning or very little learning |

working at this level, consolidation and practice of old material is the most which is likely to be achieved. This often results in a quiet lesson, but no new learning for most children. Worse, in the longer term children may become bored and disengaged, acquiring bad working and learning habits.

At the highest level, work is so far beyond the children's current level that it goes completely over their heads, resulting in off-task behaviour and no learning.

Between these two extremes lies the learning zone, the ZPD, in which children can operate only with some form of support. This may be provided by a teacher, a student, a group of students or a learning resource like a book or computer. When students are in the learning zone in an exercise phase of the lesson, working noise can be heard as children ask each other for support; teachers are kept busy asking and answering questions, and maximum learning occurs. When children are in the learning zone in an exposition or teaching phase of the lesson, support is provided through the audio-visual aids and models chosen, the metaphors and allegories selected, the examples chosen and through the questions asked by teachers and students.

One of the most common forms of support provided by teachers to help children to construct knowledge is questioning. Experienced teachers rarely give lectures. Rather, their expositions and explanations are characterized by the skilled use of oral questioning (Jones, *et al.* 2000). Clearly, oral questioning has the potential to generate assessment information for teachers and students to use to guide the teaching and learning process. However, questioning in the classroom serves a range of different purposes. Sometimes, questions are used to hold the class accountable for control purposes. At other times, the aim is to evaluate the extent to which students understand the issues at hand. However, at other times the aim is to control, engage and motivate students by allowing them to participate in the explanation by recalling and contributing facts that the teacher expects to be known.

Supporting learning through questioning is not new. The resulting interaction is sometimes referred to as Socratic dialogue, after the Greek philosopher Socrates (BC 469–399). More recently, the term 'scaffolding' (Bruner 1985) has been used to describe the support which a learner can draw from structured questioning. Experienced teachers are able to structure their questioning to lead a class through a problem, argument or justification, with most or all members of the class engaged and participating. Such a dialogue may have the teacher acting as a 'vicarious form of consciousness' (Bruner 1985, pp. 24–5) taking most of the strategic decisions and guiding progress in order to reduce the total cognitive load on the student. However, if too much of the decision-making – the hard work – is done by the teacher, and the student is left with only simple low-level recall questions to answer, then instead of teaching through questioning this reduces to attention management. Learning requires mental effort. If too much of the load is carried by the teacher, the potential for real learning is curtailed. The trick is to provide just enough support to allow students to progress through their own efforts (Tanner and Jones 2000a, b).

The scaffolding metaphor is an attractive one in many ways, reminiscent of construction on a building site. Scaffolding on a building site guides the form of an emerging structure, enabling people to work at higher levels before the structure is complete, and is removed when the building is secure. Scaffolding for the construction of knowledge is intended to act in the same way, but students are not inanimate bricks and mortar. The task is complicated by the range of personalities, opinions and backgrounds of the students, who will each create their own structures according to their own free will no matter what the intentions of the teacher (cf. Askew, *et al.* 1995).

Scaffolding on a building site is necessarily rigid, and is intended to lead to a construction predetermined by the blueprints. Scaffolding in the social context of the classroom must often be more flexible, accommodating individual free will and the personal nature of mental construction. While flexible or wobbly scaffolding may seem to be stretching the metaphor too far, scaffolding that is dynamic and responsive to the opinions and beliefs of students is more effective (Tanner 1997; Tanner and Jones 2000b; Jones and Tanner 2002). For learning to occur, there must be a degree of interaction between the learner and the teaching. However, if learning is to be more than superficial, learners must engage with the teaching in some meaningful manner, bringing something of themselves to the exchange, not merely passively receiving preformed information. We conceive of interactive teaching as demanding a degree of active participation by learners who contribute to the development of collective understanding, providing numerous opportunities for formative assessment by teachers and students (Tanner, *et al.* 2005).

Think about the last time you learned a new concept. The process is usually characterized by a period of uncertainty, when the ideas may seem a little fuzzy, as if being seen through fog. In the early stages, you are not sure whether you understand the ideas completely. If you were in a formal educational setting, perhaps at university, you might have been offered a definition to learn, but even this is not usually enough. You are never quite certain that your understanding of the key words and phrases is exactly the same as the teacher intended. How can you be sure?

The process of knowledge construction is necessarily tentative. Learners are not sure at first to what extent their version of the concept or idea being taught is valid. They need feedback. They need to find ways to test their tentative constructions against knowledge that has been officially approved. This demands a form of self-assessment by the learner – 'I think I understand what is going on . . . but how can I check?'

In school, students get formal feedback when teachers take in work for marking, but this process involves inevitable delays. Misunderstandings may have been reinforced through repetition for some considerable time before corrected work is returned. Children require regular, immediate feedback while they are striving to understand new ideas and construct new knowledge systems. They are able to test the validity of their ideas to a limited extent when listening to an exposition or reading a book, but the process is much easier and more efficient when the teaching is interactive.

The processes involved in the construction of knowledge suggest that students should have opportunities to articulate their tentative ideas. The very act of putting ideas into words forces learners to clarify their thoughts. If they are expected to explain their ideas to the rest of the class, then their ideas must be clarified still further for testing in the public domain. If the teacher has managed to develop a positive learning community, classroom discussion provides a very effective mechanism for rapid feedback and knowledge development. While discussion proceeds, learners are able to compare their ideas with those expressed by others. Often misconceptions are shared by several members of the class and teachers are able to challenge them directly when they are expressed. Experienced teachers are often able to predict the most common misconceptions in advance and may even have chosen tasks with the deliberate intention of exposing them.

Interactive teaching helps to develop shared understandings within the class. Tentative individual constructions may be tested against the shared, corporate understanding of the class, although final responsibility for the validation of ideas remains with the teacher. This process allows for rapid, informal formative assessment by students and teachers.

Ideally, a classroom culture should exist in which teachers and students can work jointly on problem-solving activities and knowledge construction in a conjecturing atmosphere. Teachers should be able to draw on their subject knowledge to identify more than one way to achieve the desired learning outcomes and hence to follow the learner's path some of the time, rather than rigidly prescribing their own (Askew, *et al.* 1995; Wood and Wood 1996; Jones, *et al.* 2000).

We conceptualize interactivity in whole-class teaching on a continuum according to the degree of teacher/student control, the nature of the interaction and the character of the scaffolding provided through the dialogue (see Figure 1.1).

The form of whole-class teaching with the lowest level of interaction and thus the least potential for formative assessment is the lecture. In lectures, there may be no interaction between the cognitive processes of the student and the teaching. Any interaction is internal as some learners may try to compare their ideas with what is being said. Although this is under the control of the student, it does not influence the development of the lesson, which remains under the control of the teacher. Scaffolding is restricted to the

| Nature of the Interaction | Control |
| --- | --- |
| ● Lecture | High degree of teacher control |
| *No interactivity or only internal interactivity* | |
| ● Low level/funnelling questioning | |
| *Rigid scaffolding and surface interactivity* | |
| ● Probing questioning | |
| *Looser scaffolding and deeper interactivity* | |
| ● Focusing or uptake questioning | |
| *Dynamic scaffolding and deep interactivity* | |
| ● Collective reflection | High degree of pupil control |
| *Reflective scaffolding and full interaction* | |

**Figure 1.1  Interaction in Whole Class Teaching** (Tanner, *et al.* 2005)

selective use by the teacher of metaphors, allegories, and diagrams, etc. which are intended to contact and support students' cognitive processes. Formative assessment opportunities are very limited.

The second level in our hierarchy of interaction utilizes a rigid form of scaffolding based on simple, low-level, funnelling questioning (Bauersfeld 1988). In funnelling, it is the teacher who selects the thinking strategies and controls the decision-making process to lead the discourse to a predetermined solution. Research suggests that this is the most common form of interaction, with most teachers' questions demanding short, factual responses of a relatively low cognitive level, designed to funnel students' responses towards a required answer (Burns and Myhill 2004; Smith, *et al.* 2004). Assessment in this context is quite limited as students' contributions are often restricted to secure knowledge that is presumed to be widely known already. Few opportunities are available for students to test their own ideas, other than internally.

The third level is based on a looser form of scaffolding in which an individual student's contribution to the interaction is given greater prominence as the teacher extends and sustains the dialogue through probing questions, allowing for formative assessment decisions to be made by both students and teachers. Contributions by children tend to be longer and more involved. Follow-up questions are often asked of individual children as teachers try to gain a deeper understanding of their ideas. Through their more sustained involvement in formative assessment, students begin to gain some degree of control over the interaction, albeit within a loose funnelling structure orchestrated by the teacher. Although formative assessment based on such rich questioning is linked to improved performance (Black and Wiliam 1998a, b), probing questioning occurs infrequently in English classrooms (Smith, *et al.* 2004, p. 408).

In contrast to the rigid scaffolding provided by funnelling questions, the next level in our hierarchy is based on a more dynamic form of scaffolding in which students and teachers interact more collaboratively to develop a shared understanding in the class about the issue or problem in question (Tanner and Jones 2000a). The aim is to develop a discussion around a problem or issue in which differences in perspective are welcomed and encouraged. In the ensuing discussion, learners are required to express their ideas orally for testing in debate. This requires a sufficiently rich question or issue to be presented that leaves room for alternative perspectives to be taken, and a classroom culture that leads students to believe that their opinions are valued. As the discussion proceeds, the class begins to develop a form of shared understanding as they construct knowledge together.

The most significant participant in the discussion remains the teacher, who validates conjectures and uses focusing questions to control its general direction. Focusing questions draw the attention of the class to aspects of students' contributions that are important. For example, attention might be drawn to strategies, explanations, helpful insights or features of the problem that are not yet understood. The class then evaluate strategies and explanations; resolve collectively any perturbations that have been created; or take up new ideas and develop them further (Wood 1994, p. 160).

Such scaffolding is flexible and unpredictable, demanding a high level of skill and confidence from teachers who must think on their feet in response to conjectures, strategies and explanations suggested by students, picking up their ideas and incorporating them into the discussion. However, in return, students are provided with many opportunities to test the validity of their ideas in a public domain. It also affords opportunities for the teacher to identify misconceptions and to adjust teaching accordingly (Tanner and Jones 2000b).

Although the National Strategies for Key Stage 2 (DfES 2005a) and Key Stage 3 (DfES 2005b) encourage discussion of students' own ideas through interactive teaching, recent research suggests that uptake questioning, in which a student's response is incorporated into the ongoing discourse, is uncommon, occurring in less than 5 per cent of exchanges, with nearly half (43 per cent) of teachers never using the strategy (Smith, *et al.* 2004, p. 408).

The highest level in our hierarchy is based on collective reflection (Cobb, *et al.* 1997; Tanner 1997). The focus of this form of interaction is on evaluation and reflection and encourages effective formative assessment by students and teachers. It usually occurs when teachers deliberately generate a reflective discussion after activities, perhaps in a plenary session, to encourage self-evaluation and reflection on the learning that has occurred. Many different activities may be used to generate a reflective discourse, including, for example, peer and self-assessment; students writing their own revision notes; students writing their own examination questions; students acting as rapporteurs, etc. We will be discussing such strategies in Chapter 4. Research indicates that the use of reflective strategies is effective in helping children to formalize their newly acquired knowledge, often linking it to older knowledge and making it more easily transferable to new situations (Tanner and Jones 2000a).

Teaching in secondary schools is heavily influenced by the Key Stage 3 National Strategy (DfES 2005b). This developed from the Literacy and Numeracy Strategies for Key Stage 2 (DfEE 1998; 1999). In secondary schools in England, subject Strategies now exist in English, mathematics, science, ICT and modern foreign languages within the overall strategy for Key Stage 3. Although the official status of the Strategies is 'guidance', in England they have not been regarded as optional (Jones and Tanner 2002). They contain detailed prescriptive advice from the level of individual lessons to whole-school planning. Unfortunately, although many aspects of the Strategies have a sound theoretical basis, this is not explained or developed, and teachers are left with instructions about how to act but without any sense of an underpinning rationale. In fact, there are several tensions and contradictions inherent in the guidance that many teachers have found confusing (Mroz, *et al.* 2000, English, *et al.* 2002). For example, obvious tensions exist between:

- demands for pace versus allowing children time to think through their answers;

- demands for pace versus the development of learning and thinking skills;

- an emphasis on the rapid recall of facts versus allowing children to make extended answers in discussion;

- an emphasis on the rapid recall of facts versus formative assessment;

- fast, lively interactive teaching versus time for reflection on what has been taught;

- whole-class teaching versus personalized learning.

In the absence of any discussion about the underlying rationale for the approaches, attention often tends to be focused on the superficial aspects of the Strategies.

In most subjects, lessons are intended to follow a standard format of three phases, incorporating a starter, a main teaching activity and a plenary. Attention has often been focused on these superficial structural aspects of lessons at the expense of more significant factors associated with the interactions between teachers and students. As you might have gathered from the discussion above about how children learn, we believe that the emphasis in interactive teaching should be on formative assessment, self-evaluation and reflection to help learners to build new knowledge and validate it. Fortunately, it is in the nature of interaction that the exchange of information should be a two-way process in which teachers are able to continuously assess children, evaluate the success of their teaching and feed that information forward into their planning for future exchanges.

The teaching style encouraged by the Strategies is intended to be highly interactive.

> High-quality direct teaching is oral, interactive and lively. It is not achieved by adopting a simplistic formula of 'drill and practice' and lecturing the class, or by expecting students to teach themselves from books. It is a two-way process in which students are expected to play an active part by answering questions, contributing points to discussions, and explaining and demonstrating their methods to the class. (DfEE 2001, 1.26)

Rather than a return to traditional approaches, the Strategies are intended to encourage a form of whole-class teaching that promotes higher quality dialogue, discussion and strategic thinking. Unfortunately, the mixed messages from the Strategies and the failure to explain the rationale often lead to this aim not being realized. In fact, in some cases an emphasis on 'traditional' whole-class teaching and demands for pace may be undermining the development of a more reflective and strategic approach to thinking (Kyriacou and Goulding 2004).

Interactive teaching requires the effective use of informal, continuous assessment for learning but, as we indicated earlier, assessment practices in schools have traditionally emphasized its summative aspects. Black and Wiliam (1998a, pp. 17–18; 1998b) have identified a number of negative assessment practices, which they claimed were often to be found in UK schools. You might consider whether any apply to the practices in your own institution:

- test questions encourage rote and superficial learning;

- the giving of marks or grades is over-emphasized, while the giving of advice is under-emphasized;

- an over-emphasis on competition rather than personal improvement teaches low-attaining students that they lack 'ability';

- feedback often serves social and managerial functions, at the expense of learning functions;

- teachers are often able to predict students' results on external tests because their own tests imitate them, but at the same time they know too little about their students' learning needs;

- the collection of marks to fill up records is given greater priority than the analysis of students' work to discern learning needs.

The criticisms above are associated with a failure to use assessment effectively to support learning. The first home of assessment for learning is the classroom and it is on assessment in the classroom that this book is focused.

We hope that this book will help you to analyse your current practices with a view to refocusing the substantial effort and energy that you expend on assessment more closely on students' learning. Considerable research evidence exists that practices loosely described as 'assessment for learning' can lead to significant gains in attainment (Black and Wiliam 1998a, b). We hope to introduce you to some of that research and describe some practical approaches that you can employ to get the most from your assessment.

## 2

# Formative assessment

## What do we mean by formative assessment?

Since the introduction of the National Curriculum, the major purpose for assessment has been to hold teachers, schools and LEAs to account. Managerial and communicative functions have dominated and formative assessment initially received comparatively little attention (Daugherty 1995).

However, a highly influential systematic review of research conducted into formative assessment has demonstrated that high-quality formative assessment has a powerful impact on learning (Black and Wiliam 1998a, b). The size of the effect found in the international studies, they reported, was so large that if it were applied to all schools the improvement in performance would be sufficient to lift England from 41st to 5th place in the international league tables developed in the Third International Mathematics and Science Study (TIMSS: Beaton, et al. 1996). For the average student, it would amount to an improvement of two grades at GCSE. Low attainers are reported to benefit even more, with an increase of three grades in comparison, with one grade for higher attainers. Unfortunately, the research also shows that high-quality formative assessment is not very common (Black and Wiliam 1998b).

Of course, much depends on what we mean by formative assessment. Black and Wiliam interpreted the term to encompass

All those activities undertaken by teachers, and/or by their students, which provide information to be used as feedback to modify the teaching and learning activities in which they are engaged. (Black and Wiliam 1998a)

The terms 'formative' and 'summative' are not used consistently in the literature. The terms are often used as if they describe different *types* of assessment: however, we prefer to use the terms to describe the *functions* of it.

We use the term 'assessment event' to describe the culture, expectations and actions associated with an assessment activity. This includes the preparation for the assessment by both the teacher and the student, the feedback from the assessment offered by the teacher, the nature of any analysis or reflection on the assessment by teachers or students and the impact of the assessment on subsequent learning and teaching behaviours (cf. Brookhart 2001).

Whenever assessment occurs, the potential exists for a skilled teacher to use the event to emphasize its formative functions, even if its prime purpose was essentially summative. Much depends on teacher and learner expectations and behaviours before and after the event and the way in which feedback information is used. The issue is not whether the assessment is formal or informal, externally imposed or devised by the teacher, high stakes or low stakes. The issue is whether the potential formative functions of the assessment are exploited or not.

More recently, formative assessment has been characterized as 'assessment *for* learning', in contrast to summative assessment which is described as 'assessment *of* learning'. However, although the definition of assessment for learning offered by the Qualifications and Curriculum Authority (QCA) now pays greater regard to the learning process, it retains some of the flavour of more summative approaches.

It is rooted in self-referencing; a student needs to know where s/he is and understand not only where s/he wants to be but also how to 'fill the gap'. This involves both the teacher and the student in a process of continual reflection and review about progress. (QCA 2001a)

Our discussion of how children learn from assessment in Chapter 1 leads us to applaud the emphasis on reflection and the implication that students should be involved in self-assessment. However, the metaphor of 'filling the gap' does not sit comfortably with a view of learning as the personal construction of knowledge. As might be expected, QCA are concerned with meeting externally-imposed standards and passing examinations. We are more concerned with the quality of learning.

The current emphasis on targets and learning outcomes carries with it a danger that education becomes focused on aspects of learning that are easy to specify and measure, at the expense of other more important aspects. Clearly, schools should ensure that children are well-prepared to succeed in gaining qualifications. However, we believe that qualifications are not, in themselves, the main objective of education. Success in examination is only one of the indicators of effective learning and should not be the main aim of a good education. For example, we wish to enthuse our students with a love of our subject for its own sake and encourage them to continue to study it in later life. Furthermore, there are many important aspects of learning that are difficult to assess reliably and are often not included in external high-stakes examinations. It is helpful at this point to define our terms and distinguish clearly between reliability and validity in assessment.

'Reliability' is essentially concerned with the extent to which assessment procedures give consistent results. 'Validity', on the other hand, is the accord between what is being measured and what someone thinks the assessment ought to be measuring (Wiliam 1992). The distinction may be seen in the following example.

There is a small correlation between height and intelligence test results. If I wish to measure the intelligence of the students in my class I could measure their heights to a high degree of accuracy. This assessment would be very *reliable*, as my results would be consistent and other assessors measuring the intelligence of my students in this way would gain very similar results. However, the *validity* of the assessment is highly suspect, as it does not measure what it claims to measure. The high reliability of the technique and its ease of application might, however, make it very attractive to politicians trying to set clear and achievable standards.

Clearly, we would like our assessments of our students to be both reliable and valid, but a tension often exists between these objectives, which is difficult to resolve. For managerial purposes such as selection, high reliability is usually paramount. For formative purposes, associated with learning and teaching, high validity should be more important.

High-stakes examinations exert a backwash effect on the curriculum, with teachers and students often tending to focus on questions and tasks in the same style as the examination. The extent to which this is valid depends on the quality of the examination and your aims as a teacher. As experienced teachers, we are well aware of a range of tricks and techniques that we use to good effect in the last few weeks before high-stakes external examinations to ensure that our students gain the best grades possible. However, they do not form the basis of our day-to-day teaching approaches!

A tension often exists between learning facts without understanding and the development of coherent, systematic knowledge of a subject. The former strategy may sometimes be effective as a last resort when 'cramming' just before an examination, but it is rarely a successful strategy in the longer term; knowledge crammed in this way is usually superficial and short-lived. Good formative assessment in the classroom should usually focus on the big concepts and ideas in your subject, with the aim of developing knowledge that is integrated, deeply understood, personally meaningful and consequently memorable.

Good formative assessment should focus on the development of personal meaning and purposeful self-motivated learning rather than the meeting of standards. A side effect of this strategy is likely to be improved performance in examinations! However, although we do not regard external examinations as an end in themselves, we are in agreement with QCA that effective formative assessment represents a key strategy for raising standards. QCA advise that formative assessment, or 'assessment *for* learning' must:

- be embedded in the teaching and learning process of which it is an essential part;

- share learning goals with students;

- help students to know and to recognize the standards to aim for;

- provide feedback which leads students to identify what they should do next to improve;

- have a commitment that every student can improve;

- involve both teacher and students reviewing and reflecting on students' performance and progress;

- involve students in self-assessment. (QCA 2001a)

Although expressed in the language of goals and standards, at the heart of the advice is an emphasis on feedback that will allow students and teachers to reflect on and to improve the learning and teaching that has occurred. All the aspects of formative assessment encouraged by QCA above will be discussed in the chapters that follow, but we will focus first on ways in which formative assessment can support the teaching and learning process itself.

Both teachers and students require feedback information if teaching and learning is to proceed effectively. In Chapter 1 we looked closely at students' needs for assessment, and only briefly mentioned the teacher's need to make continuous, approximate, informal and temporary assessments to maintain students within their zones of proximal development. Now we will consider these needs in more detail.

## Informal formative assessment to support whole-class teaching

The National Strategy for Key Stage 3 is based on the direct teaching of the whole class. Grouping students by ability is encouraged by the Strategy to facilitate such an approach. However, even when a rigid setting regime is in force, a tension inevitably exists between treating the whole class as a unit and the needs of individual students.

Whole-class teaching is only possible through the effective use of formative assessment. While teaching the whole class, formative assessment is an ongoing and informal activity as you absorb and react to the way the class is responding. You can assess students' understanding in a variety of ways – by observing their facial expressions, looking at their written work, asking questions, listening to students' ideas, supporting discussions, observing activities, and providing just enough support for students to progress. In response to such continuous informal assessments, you adapt your teaching, speeding up or slowing down the pace, introducing a new metaphor, making continuous judgements and decisions about how to proceed.

At the start of a lesson or unit of work, informal baseline assessment helps you to judge the extent of existing knowledge and determine exactly where to pitch the lesson. Even where previous records exist, it is wise to fine-tune your teaching by assessing exactly how much they are able to recall today! If previous learning was superficial rather than deep, it may have decayed since the record was made. Such informal assessments also act as scene-setting, reminding students of earlier work and contextualizing today's work. Baseline assessment may also include the identification of common misconceptions or difficulties.

As the main teaching activity progresses, formative assessment and fine-tuning continues though judicious use of questioning, observation, listening and discussion. Most lessons include a phase in which students are released from direct teaching of the whole class to participate in individual or group work, performing an activity, practising a skill or completing an exercise. Again, immediate informal feedback is necessary to help you judge whether they have understood the issues sufficiently to begin such work. A distinctive feature of lesson-planning associated with formative assessment is its flexibility (Torrance and Prior 1998, p. 155).

Finally, at the end of the session, it is necessary to assess the extent to which they have understood the key issues, with a view to evaluating the success of your teaching and planning the next lesson.

Your problem throughout all of these phases is that you must make continuous, rapid, approximate assessments of the understanding and progress of each individual student. Much of your feedback information will have been provided by oral questioning of the whole class. Unfortunately, some students will have been more inclined to respond to questioning than others. In fact, some students may not have volunteered to answer a single question while others have called out answers many times! Questioning must be managed both to ensure classroom control and to gain adequate feedback from *all* students.

The traditional use of 'hands up' to signal that a student wishes to respond also gives an indication of the proportion of the class that think they can answer. You then sample the accuracy of their self-assessments by nominating who answers. The danger here is that some students will decide not to put their hands up. Not only does this allow some students not to participate fully in the lesson, but also it leaves you with inadequate and incomplete feedback information.

Current advice from QCA (2005) is to abandon 'hands up' as an indicator that a student wishes to answer a question, but to reserve it for when a student wishes to ask a question. Teachers should always nominate which student is to answer rather than take volunteers. This risks embarrassing students by asking them questions they cannot answer. In some school cultures such public failure may be extremely humiliating.

Perhaps the greatest danger involved in abandoning 'hands up' is that in your desire to avoid the potential problem of embarrassing students, you limit your interaction by only asking easy, short-answer questions. Strong discipline and a safe, supportive classroom culture must be developed before the abandoning of 'hands up' is practical and we suggest that you make your own judgement according to your circumstances.

One strategy that might help you to move towards 'hands down' in a safe, supportive learning culture is to amend the questioning routine as follows:

- Ask a rich question of all the class and allow time for them to think in silence as individuals.

- Ask them to discuss their thinking with the person next to them.

- Choose several different groups to comment and make no judgement on their replies, perhaps noting their comments on the board.

- Generate a whole-class discussion about an ideal solution, focusing attention on the solution rather than individual student contributions. (Tanner and Jones 1994; 1995)

Some novice teachers try to gain continuous feedback on their teaching by asking 'Do you all understand?' This is an ineffective strategy for a number of reasons. First, the question begs the answer 'Yes' whether it is true or not. Confessing to not under-standing in public may not be socially acceptable, particularly if you think that most of your classmates do understand. Second, students can only really judge whether they understand an idea when they have to apply it in a context. It is up to the teacher to ask a rich question to expose any misconceptions.

Whole-class feedback can also be gained by asking students to indicate whether they understand or not by putting thumbs up, down or sideways to indicate yes, no and maybe. A similar strat-egy involves 'traffic light' cards of red, amber and green that can be shown in the palm of the hand, maintaining privacy. However, these strategies seem to us to suffer from both the problems listed above, although perhaps a sideways thumb is easier to offer than complete misunderstanding. More importantly, they do not address the problem that students are not aware of their genuine misconceptions. It is in the nature of a misconception that you believe that you understand completely. It is only when a teacher poses a sufficiently rich question that you begin to realize that there is something wrong.

## How can 'rich questioning' support informal formative assessment?

There has been considerable research into the precise nature of children's misconceptions since the mid-1970s. Early large-scale research studies include Concepts in Secondary Mathematics and Science (CSMS) (Hart 1981) and the work of the Assessment of Performance Unit (APU) (Foxman 1985). These and subsequent studies (e.g. Stigler, *et al.* 1999; Ryan and Williams 2000; Stacey 2005) have helped us to understand the misconceptions that chil-dren commonly hold in certain key areas of the curriculum, and the thinking that leads them to offer incorrect responses in par-ticular circumstances.

Most of the research into misconceptions has been conducted in mathematics and science, due to the clear conceptual basis and the more absolute nature of 'truth' in those subjects. However, all subjects have concepts that must be understood in a deep, meaningful manner, as well as facts and conventions that must be learned, and so the principles established in these studies are generally applicable in most teaching situations.

One of the key messages from such studies is that wrong answers are not usually the result of carelessness or lack of effort, but are often the result of thinking based on unsound or insufficiently elaborated concepts. Consider, for example, this question taken from the APU study:

Circle the smallest value:

0.375    0.25    0.5    0.125

The response rates of 11 year olds to this question were:

34%    2%    43%    17%

(Foxman 1985, p. 56)

The first main error which the APU identified was a tendency to ignore the decimal point. Most of the students who considered 0.5 to be the smallest value were probably thinking that 5 is less than 125. However, another common misconception revealed by the research was that many students believe that the more digits there are after the decimal point, the smaller the number becomes. By this logic the smallest number must be 0.375 or 0.125. Thus some of the students who answered 0.125 correctly might have held the misconception that longer numbers are smaller. Unfortunately, children who base their work on false ideas may still obtain correct answers if the questions they are attempting are chosen unwisely.

Other misconceptions are based on the over-generalization of a rule that works in limited circumstances. For example, 'to multiply a number by 10, just add a nought'. This rule works for whole numbers and is sometimes deliberately taught in primary school. Unfortunately, it fails when the example chosen is a decimal, such as

$$2.3 \times 10 = ?$$

where the answer 2.30 is clearly incorrect.

Similarly, a common misconception in science is that if a body is in motion, there must be a force in the direction of that motion. Experience in the real-life world of friction and air resistance often reinforces that misconception.

Asking children, who hold such misconceptions, to indicate whether they understand is not productive. They will not volunteer that they do not understand because they probably believe that they *do* understand. It is only when they are presented with situations in which their misconception regularly leads to an incorrect answer that they begin to develop a sense of unease about their understanding. Changing the way you think about something requires mental effort – it is hard work – and consequently people do not change their ways of thinking lightly. Misconceptions are very resilient and many adults continue to hold misconceptions about topics that are taught in lower secondary school. For learning to occur:

- the students need to appreciate that something is not quite right – to have a sense of unease about their current understanding;

- the learning process needs to be important enough to the students for them to make the effort to change;

- just telling them is not enough – students need help in order to construct new knowledge and to connect it to their existing concepts. (Tanner and Jones 2000b)

Being asked the right question is a critical first step in developing a sense of unease about your current thinking. The difficulty for the teacher is that knowledge of children's thinking depends on asking good questions but it is only by understanding how students think that we begin to understand the nature of a good question.

> It is only by asking the right, probing questions that we discover deep misconceptions, and it is only by knowing which misconceptions are likely that we know which questions are worth asking. (Swan 1983, p. 65)

So how can you break into this loop and make your questioning richer? First, we advise you to read any research into children's misconceptions that exists in your subject area. Even experienced teachers are sometimes surprised by what research interviews have revealed to be going on in children's heads! We believe strongly that reading the research on misconceptions in your subject should be a key component in courses of initial teacher education and training. Second, we advise you to listen very carefully to your students' explanations of their thinking!

During their planning, good teachers anticipate exactly what their students are likely to misunderstand. You are able to predict some misconceptions for yourself by reflecting on the topic being taught and imagining yourself in the place of the student. Asking the advice of more experienced teachers or discussing children's errors in departmental meetings will help you to identify others. However, it is possible to develop your questioning skills through experience if you provide students with opportunities to expose their misconceptions by asking sufficiently rich questions and encouraging them to explain their thinking in detail.

As we indicated above, getting an answer correct does not prove conclusively that a concept is completely understood. We like the metaphor of trying to sail a boat through an unfamiliar channel. If you hit a rock then you know that you have made a mistake but a successful passage gives you little information about what lies underwater or whether you have taken the best route. Similarly, a student may achieve the correct answer to a problem through the use of a limited or inefficient strategy. The answer alone will not alert you to an underlying misconception; further interaction and extended commentary by the student is necessary to elicit the thinking. You should note that the researchers in CSMS and APU developed their insights into misconceptions by interviewing children, engaging with rich questions and probing their ways of thinking. Insight into misconceptions and the development of a rich questioning style depends on listening carefully to children explaining their thinking, and focusing on the way *they* see the situation rather than simply telling them how you would like them to think. When you identify a misconception, you are then able to present them with examples, situations and arguments that confront it directly, forcing them to recognize the need to restructure their thoughts.

If you are unsure of the range of misconceptions that might exist in a particular topic, it is often helpful to generate discussion and argumentation in your class to reveal children's thinking. In order for a question to be effective as a stimulus for such a discussion, it must be sufficiently open to include a *problematic*, that is an 'unresolved or not trivially resolvable problem', which induces sufficient purpose or tension to sustain a discussion (Ryan and Williams 2000). Problems may often be developed from the common misconceptions, which occur in all subjects. 'Rumours' is a useful device for creating discussions based on such misconceptions. For example:

- I heard a rumour the other day that glaciers retreat back up hill during the summer. What do you think? Why?

- I heard a rumour that multiplication always gives you a bigger answer. What do you think? Is it always true?

- I heard a rumour that Icarus flew so high that the sun melted his wings and he crashed to the ground. Do you think this would be likely to happen? Why?

We often like to use such rumours as lesson starters, asking students to think about the rumour in silence for a couple of minutes before discussing it with their neighbour or a small group of other students. Students are then selected to present a reasoned case to the class, without judgement or validation by the teacher. This can generate rich dialogue and open a window into students' thinking, revealing misconceptions and encouraging extended discussion.

The aim is to expose a wide range of misconceptions for discussion and validation in the public domain. Misconceptions should be challenged through debate with other students where possible, but the ensuing discussion should be supported and developed through questioning by the teacher. This should be indirect in character, so as not to steal the problem by funnelling thinking. A sufficient problem must be left for students to solve using their own powers of reasoning.

Concepts which are not yet fully elaborated or connected to existing knowledge should be strengthened through argumentation and discussion. The teacher can support this through focusing questions and encouragement to engage in collective reflection. The resulting dialogue should be thoughtful, reflective and intended to explore understanding, giving all students the opportunity to think and to articulate their thoughts (Tanner 1997; Black and Wiliam 1998b). QCA offers the following examples of questions, which can be effective in providing assessment opportunities:

- How can we be sure that . . .?

- Is it ever/always true/false that . . .?

- Why do _, _, _, all give the same answer?

- How do you . . .?

- How would you explain . . .?

- What does that tell us about . . .?

- What is wrong with . . .?

- Why is _ true? (QCA 2003, p. 9)

It is in the nature of rich questions that they require time for thinking and reflection before offering a considered response. Sadly, the over-emphasis on pace encouraged by the National Strategies is leading teachers to offer insufficient time for students to think and reflect fully about all the issues before responding to oral questions. In many classrooms, help is given or the question is redirected to another student if an immediate answer is not forthcoming. If the question is sufficiently rich to demand thought, then the 'wait-time' between the students' answer and the teachers' evaluation should be extended to allow the student to reflect and expand on their answer. Wiliam (1999a, p. 18) claims that extending the 'wait time' to three seconds produces measurable increases in learning without causing lessons to lose pace. We often prefer to slow things down even further by demanding that all students engage with the issue in silence for a minute before sharing ideas with a neighbour and finally initiating whole-class discussion.

The new learning that has been prompted by rich questioning may be reflected on further during the plenary. Plenaries provide excellent opportunities for formative assessment by students and teachers. Students often find that although they thought they understood each stage that the lesson passed through, it is a step further in learning to gather all the pieces together into a coherent whole. The realization of this is often when students are asked to summarize the main points of the lesson for themselves. At this stage, teachers may find self-assessment devices such as traffic light cards useful to judge the success of their teaching.

However, a more productive strategy is to generate dialogues in which students offer their own summaries to the class to be adapted and strengthened through discussion and collective reflection, guided by focusing questions from the teacher to emphasize the key points. Engaging in such collective reflection in a plenary helps students to formalize the knowledge they have gained and is associated with significant increases in learning (Tanner and Jones 2000a). Dialogues generated during plenaries provide further opportunities for formative assessment, helping teachers to evaluate their teaching and to begin to plan for the next lesson, and helping students to identify their strengths and to set personal targets for further learning.

## Formal versus informal target-setting

The informal, dynamic assessments that support effective learning and teaching in the fast-moving interactive classroom are not formally recorded. There is no point – if they are effective they should be out of date before the end of the lesson!

The assessments that occur in the plenary are of a slightly different character. Although we expect their function to be largely formative, in that they help teachers to plan their next lesson and students to set their immediate targets for future learning, they have some summative characteristics. A plenary can offer an opportunity to pause, reflect and evaluate at the end of a discrete unit of learning. It allows for self-referencing by the teacher, identifying the stage the class have reached in their learning so far, relating that to the learning outcomes for the module, and devising strategies for progression (cf. QCA 2001a).

Plenaries also provide opportunities for self-referencing by students, who should have been guided through rich questioning, discussion and reflection to identify what they know they understand and what they still feel a sense of unease about. Whether this can be expressed as a personal target for future learning will depend on the nature of the learning that is required. Factual information, for example: 'Learn the definition of a drainage basin', is easily expressed as a target, but developing the deeper, conceptual understanding necessary to explain the processes through which drainage basins operate is far more difficult to express as a target.

Since 1997 the government has attempted to manage change in the public services through the imposition of targets. Consequently, many of the managerial functions of assessment are expressed in the language of targets. National targets have been imposed in terms of percentages of students attaining key benchmarks, such as level 5 at Key Stage 3 and five A* to C grades at GCSE. Although such targets were set with the intention of raising standards, it is doubtful whether their impact is entirely benign. The more significant the achievement of a target, the more distorting is its impact. League tables of schools based on the five A* to C grades benchmark place an artificial premium on the performance of students near the C/D grade boundary. Improving a student's grade from E to D, or from B to A, achieves nothing in league-table terms. Resources are often targeted at students who are on the C/D borderline, in the hope of gaining more C grades. This inevitably disadvantages other groups (Gillborn and Youdell 2000, pp. 133–65).

Targets for schools and for teachers are usually expressed in terms of the proportion of students gaining such benchmark grades. In the best practice, such targets are negotiated in the light of professional knowledge about the individual students and involve discussion of strategies that might improve learning. However, in many cases they are simply imposed.

Students are at the bottom end of a very long chain of imposed and negotiated targets. The process of target-setting for students is often distorted by the managerial functions of target-setting imposed further up the chain. Target-setting for students should fulfil a very different purpose. A distinction must be made between *performance* targets and *process* targets.

Performance targets are associated with the achievement of specified, measurable outcomes, such as the percentage of students gaining five A* to C grades at GCSE. They aim to hold

35

teachers and schools accountable and raise pass rates. Performance targets are transmitted down through the system to impinge eventually on teachers and classes.

Process targets, on the other hand, relate to specific actions that are to be taken. In education they are often expressed as *learning* targets and tend to be more personal, shorter term and associated with knowledge and understanding. It is process targets that may be useful to students in improving their learning.

Unfortunately, students are often set performance targets based on their previous results, perhaps using value-added analyses. Such targets are often set in terms of a grade to be gained in an examination. In reality, such targets are little more than an exhortation to try harder. They are too broad and long-term to engage with effectively. They cannot be adapted into shorter-term achievable sub-goals, without significant teacher support. Performance targets tend to encourage students to focus on attaining the grade, rather than developing understanding.

Performance targets also encourage students to make comparisons with other, higher-attaining students. When based on value-added data and previous performance, they include implicit assumptions about ability being innate. How motivated would you feel if you were told at the start of Year 7 that your target was to gain a grade D at GCSE? As we will discuss further in Chapter 5, if students are to be motivated to learn, they must be discouraged from regarding their performance as being based on some form of innate natural ability which is fixed and unchangeable (Brookes 2002, p. 52). Students must become convinced that effort on their part will lead to progress.

Process targets which are focused on learning are claimed to lead to higher motivation and achievement than performance targets (Black and Wiliam 1998a, p. 14). However, research into the impact of target-setting on learning is ambiguous. When students have been actively involved in the target-setting process and challenging but achievable targets are coupled with regular progress reviews, they are claimed to be effective (Brooks 2002, p. 52). Similarly, Clarke (1998, p. 96) claims that when the targets are personal and clearly relate to individuals, children can be motivated by them. However, in many schools there is a large discrepancy between the rhetoric and the reality of teachers' and students' practices (Bullock and Wikeley 2001, p. 69). In many schools, the target-setting process is erratic, bureaucratic and time consuming, with little or no evidence of any improvement in learning. Students report that targets are set, but that they are seldom monitored or their achievement recognized (Weeden, *et al.* 2002, pp. 50–1). When targets are not perceived as being owned by students and are not reviewed regularly, they quickly become meaningless and demotivating (Bullock and Wikeley 2001, p. 69).

Unfortunately, we suspect that the dynamics of school life are such that any *formal* process of target setting is likely to suffer from these criticisms. The time required for negotiation to ensure that targets are personally meaningful is unlikely to be available. Similarly, formal targets are unlikely to reviewed regularly.

The DfEE (1997, p. 10) claims that the key to effective target setting is to think SMART. Targets should be Specific, Measurable, Achievable, Realistic and Time-related. However, like most acronyms, we think that it misses the point. We think that there are more important criteria which should be fulfilled:

- Targets should focus on learning rather than performance.

- Targets should be personal.

- Target-setting should be seen as an aspect of formative assessment and planned to be an integral part of the teaching and learning process.

- Targets should be frequently monitored and reviewed.

- They should be achievable in the short-term.

- Students must want to achieve them.

- Students should participate in setting targets, and have a sense of ownership of the targets. (Tanner and Jones 2003c, p. 69).

A formal process of target-setting that fulfilled these criteria would be very time consuming, and while it would be possible to prioritize the process at the expense of other activity, the ambiguous nature of the research evidence makes us doubt that this is the best use of resources.

We do not doubt, however, the value of asking children to reflect on and evaluate their work, identifying their own learning needs. Nor do we doubt the value of teachers providing regular feedback that offers children advice on how to improve their learning. But such activities should be informal in character and part of the normal day-to-day feedback and marking strategies that are planned to be a part of a systematic process of formative assessment.

# 3

# Feedback and marking strategies

## Planning for assessment in the short, medium and long term

As we indicated in the last chapter, children should be asked to pause to reflect on and evaluate their learning on a regular basis. Reflection is supposed to underpin the target-setting process and, in the best practice, target-setting meetings are reflective. However, reflection alone is not enough – action-planning should result.

When target-setting is based on long-term aspirations and performance rather than learning, the danger is that targets will be more like New Year resolutions rather than specific action plans. If target-setting is to stimulate intellectual development, then learning tasks, assessment techniques and feedback must all be planned to challenge misconceptions, support reflection and help students to identify clear steps towards the re-structuring of ideas.

You should realize by now that assessment is not something that can just happen in a haphazard way, but should be planned for. Indeed it is as important to plan assessment as it is to plan teaching. They are opposite sides of the same coin and should be planned together.

In order to be able to teach and assess effectively, you need to be clear about your aims. By this we mean more than giving clear learning outcomes for teaching episodes. It is easy to fall into the trap of reducing your subject to a list of detailed learning objectives that can be assessed easily, but to lose sight of your long-term aims for teaching your subject. The assessment regime in your classroom ought to reflect your beliefs about learning and teaching and the nature of your subject.

The prevailing assessment regime has a major influence on the development of the attitudes and norms of behaviour that form the basis of the learning culture in your classroom. Many powerful cognitive and emotional messages are conveyed through the ways that you assess your students and you should think very carefully about the messages that you are sending. Assessment provides information, but for whom? Is it aimed at providing feedback information to students so that they can modify their learning, or is it aimed at collecting data for records and reporting to others? Is assessment done *for* students or *to* students?

It is not possible to formally assess everything that a student does. You have to select key skills, knowledge and concepts as indicators of learning. At a very practical level, you have to decide *what* you assess, *when* you assess it and *how* you assess it. If the learning outcomes that you have planned for your lessons are sufficiently rich, they should lead you naturally to what you wish to assess. However, WYTIWYG – What You Test Is What You Get – is a helpful acronym to bear in mind when determining what to assess. What you choose to assess sends a powerful message to your class about what you value in your subject. Although you may claim to value creativity and imagination, if your assessments reward only memorization, your class will draw the obvious conclusions. We must ensure that we assess what is important rather than that which is convenient.

There is a tension here, as teachers often try to write assessment items in the style of external examination questions. Because of the high stakes nature of external examinations, these aim at high reliability rather than validity and are sometimes quite limited in scope. If your assessment is intended to serve formative aims rather than predict examination performance, you may choose to emphasize validity over reliability and provide feedback on a wider range of knowledge and skills. The dead hand of external examination should not be allowed to permeate the whole of secondary education.

When and how you assess will also depend on the precise purpose of the assessment, and whether you wish to record, predict or modify performance. If your purpose is to record performance, you should be clear about the purpose (if any) of the record. Unless reinforced by review or revision, knowledge appears to decay over time. Recorded data from previous assessments may offer only limited information about current understanding or future performance. In spite of the effort expended on them, many of the records maintained in school seem unfit for the purposes they are intended to serve (Black and Wiliam 1998a, b).

The timing, context and form of an assessment make a significant difference to its usefulness. When planning for assessment, we find it helpful to consider these issues in the short, medium and longer term.

Short-term formative assessment is dynamic and flexible in character, designed to initiate immediate, real-time changes to learning and teaching. The results are short-lived and there is little point in recording them – they should be out of date before the end of the lesson. These dynamic short-term assessments fall into three broad categories: baseline, concurrent and plenary.

Informal baseline assessments usually occur at the start of the lesson as you set the scene, confirming prior knowledge and identifying misconceptions. As the lesson proceeds, concurrent formative assessment is used to fine-tune interactions, helping you to judge the minimum amount of support needed by individuals. Skilled teachers also use concurrent assessment to identify specific misconceptions that they then target with supplementary questions.

This process is flexible and dynamic, and sometimes appears to be unplanned, because there is no pre-prepared script and the exact route that the lesson will follow is not fixed in advance. Certainly there is an element of 'flying by the seat of your pants' inherent in the process when experienced teachers make themselves responsive to children's thinking. Trainee teachers sometimes mistakenly read this as suggesting that the most effective and experienced teachers do not plan their lessons. This is not the case. We refer to the form of planning involved as 'fuzzy planning'. Learning objectives and potential misconceptions are identified clearly in advance. Key 'rich questions' are selected to challenge misconceptions. Resources are prepared and pivotal points in the lesson are identified. The general trajectory of the lesson is known even if the precise path is not.

Further formative assessment should occur in the plenary. The plenary provides an opportunity for students to pause and reflect on their learning, consolidating and formalizing the knowledge they have gained and evaluating the extent to which they have achieved the learning objectives. This should also be a point where areas of unease or incomplete understanding are identified and personal learning targets are formulated. There are several plenary activities that can support such reflective formative assessment, and we will discuss these further in Chapter 4: however, most are dependent on effective feedback and support by the teacher in the form of rich questioning to stimulate discussion and the co-construction of knowledge. An effective plenary session also provides feedback to the teacher, allowing you to evaluate the success of your teaching in relation to the learning of individual students, and to plan for the next lesson.

Information for medium-term assessments may potentially come from a number of different sources. These might include: tasks completed in class or at home, marking exercise books, informal short-class tests, or more formal end-of-unit/half term/end-of-term tests. Your school or department probably has an assessment policy that details which of these sources are to be used, and the minimum frequency of assessment.

To use end-of-unit assessments formatively demands careful timing. Although, at first sight, it seems logical to assess at the end of the module, this is not helpful for formative purposes. By the time the feedback is received by the student that unit is finished and new work is being studied. There is little for the student to do but note the grade and resolve to try harder next time. To serve formative ends, assessment and feedback should occur before the end of the module, allowing students to remedy weaknesses and improve their performance while there is still time. As a student, the focus then moves away from assessment being done to you to provide grades and towards providing feedback to you to help you learn.

If the form of the assessment is more imaginative than a timed written test, perhaps involving making a presentation to the class, or writing a report on a short investigation, then formative feedback may be given via discussion of a first draft prior to final submission at the end of the module.

Medium-term assessments are commonly used to generate grades to monitor or track students' progress. The grades are often used when reporting to parents, providing evidence, for example, that a child is good at algebra but weak at geometry. The extent that such information is actually useful is at best debatable. It is not clear how the child or the parents are supposed to use such information to effect change. More finely grained data, based on detailed analysis of strategies and errors, would be required to be of use in setting effective learning targets. Unfortunately, the analysis of students' work to determine learning needs is given a low priority in most schools (Black and Wiliam 1998b, p. 6).

Some schools store such data centrally and use it to monitor or track students so that they can identify trends in performance, perhaps identifying that a child has begun to underperform across a number of subjects. Systems like this are intended to prevent students from 'falling through the net' by identifying potential problems in good time. However, it is not the records themselves that are significant, but the use that is made of them within the pastoral system.

The value of end-of-unit assessment records for predicting performance in external examination is often dubious. An assessment made immediately after teaching is likely to overestimate performance at a later date, particularly if the topic has not been revisited since. Information that has been learned in a superficial manner may be retained in the short term, but decay rapidly in the weeks that follow. Records that are to be used for prediction require an assessment of deeper, more meaningful learning. Furthermore, examining one unit at a time fails to assess whether students have made links between different topics and are able to apply knowledge in different contexts. End-of-unit tests appear to be the wrong mechanism for the purpose of prediction. Although medium-term assessments based on topics or units of work have a minor summative function, the emphasis should be placed on their formative functions and they should be timed accordingly.

Summative and predictive aims would be better served by intermittent assessments on a longer timescale. Medium-term summative assessments should include at least two or three new topics, and also periodically reassess significant key objectives from older work. Such a system could be used to encourage students to review older work periodically. Much depends on the preparation that precedes the assessment, the culture of the classroom and the extent to which revision skills are taught directly.

Currently, the primary aims of long-term assessments are often managerial in character. Students' progress may be measured against national standards or the key objectives for a key stage, allowing managers of the system to hold teachers, departments or schools accountable, or to judge the impact of an initiative. Value-added data are often used, allowing managers to monitor the performance of classes and teachers towards predicted targets.

Secondary schools usually undertake a summative assessment of their students at least once a year. These assessments are often based on the results of school tests or examinations, which summarize the work of the year or the term. These examinations are often very formal, time consuming, disrupt the timetable, and represent a significant event in students' school lives.

It is often claimed that end-of-year summative assessments provide useful information about standards for the next teachers of the students. Sadly, the information provided by end-of-year examinations is rarely in a form that would aid the planning of a new teacher taking over the class.

The precise purpose of end-of-year examinations is not always clear, beyond providing an apparently objective item to include on a school report! They may also be used to justify allocating a student to a particular ability set or course. However, you might question whether the time and emotion invested in such examinations is worth the effort for such limited purposes. Surely good teachers should know their students well enough to discuss their progress with parents or to judge if they are misplaced in a class?

When school examinations have high status, they can motivate some children to revise work, although few know how to do this effectively without significant intervention from teachers. There is also evidence that when the focus is on competition and comparisons between students, there is a negative impact on the development of some groups of students. While competition can be a powerful motivator, the losers in the competition often begin to believe that they lack natural ability, leading them to 'retire hurt', losing the motivation to learn (Black 1998b, p. 43). Much depends on whether the assessment culture in the school is focused on performance or learning.

We are not arguing that long-term summative assessment is unimportant – far from it! Assessment by single topic is insufficiently challenging and fails to encourage students to consolidate learning from different topics over time. Furthermore, in order to maintain a sense of direction and purpose, learners need to stand back and take stock at regular intervals. However, many secondary school examination and recording systems still suffer from an absence of educational purpose. The collection of marks to fill up records is often given a higher priority than the analysis of students' work to discern learning needs (Black and Wiliam 1998b, p. 6). Ofsted (1998, p. 93) reported that although the recording of student progress was improving, the results were generally underused, which suggests that sadly in many schools, summative assessment and recording remains an end in itself rather than an aid to learning.

Although the primary purpose of longer term assessment is often seen as summative, it is possible for longer term assessments and examinations to serve formative purposes. Much depends on the revision and note-taking skills that children are taught to use in preparation beforehand, and the analysis of results and feedback that occurs after the examination. We will discuss the teaching of revision strategies and the use of examinations to support learning in Chapter 5.

Longer term assessments such as yearly examinations should represent the culmination of an assessment and learning strategy based on short- and medium-term formative assessments. The form and timing of such assessments and the feedback provided contribute significantly to the development of the learning culture within your school, department or classroom. If assessment is to support learning and produce the gains described in the research literature, then the culture should emphasize learning rather than performance; personal improvement rather than competition; and developmental rather than innate ability (Black and Wiliam 1998a, b). Much of this depends on the form of feedback offered to students when assessing their written work.

## What kind of feedback do students need?

Although significant feedback occurs in real time in the two-way process of interactive teaching, inevitably much individual feedback is based on the assessment and monitoring of students' written tasks, exercises, tests and examinations. Although some feedback may be given orally during lessons while the work is progressing, inevitably much of the assessment of children's work occurs outside the classroom, and the feedback is often provided in written form, through marking.

If marking and its associated feedback is not planned effectively, it can easily lose its formative qualities and degenerate into checking whether work has been completed and presented well, or the checking of low-level facts. In fact, analysis of 131 research studies on feedback by Kluger and DeNisi (1996) showed that although on average there was a strong positive impact, in roughly 40 per cent of studies, the effect was negative. The form of feedback, the use made of it and the culture of the classroom makes a significant difference.

Black and Wiliam (1998a) claim that if assessment is to serve formative purposes, then certain key components must be present in the feedback:

- a clear indication of the nature of a perfect answer;

- information about the standard actually achieved;

- advice about how the gap might be closed;

- monitoring of the student's response to the advice in future work. (Adapted from Sadler 1989, p. 121; Black and Wiliam 1998a, p. 48).

Your interpretation of their first criterion is likely to depend on the nature of your subject and the task that you are imagining. In many closed tasks, the nature of a perfect answer may be relatively unproblematic for a student to interpret. However, in more open-ended tasks, such as coursework investigations, determining the nature of a good solution may be a significant issue. The second and third components are expressed in terms that suggest externally imposed benchmarks or examinations rather than learning for its own sake. We prefer to emphasize the need for a clear expression of the strengths and limitations of the work, an indication of how it might be improved, and a suggested strategy for change.

We doubt the value of providing feedback in terms of externally imposed benchmarks such as National Curriculum levels in the context of short- or medium-term assessment events. Individual students who have a high commitment to the goal and who believe that their chances of success are high may be motivated to learn when feedback suggests that they do not meet the external standard. However, others will choose to abandon the attempt, particularly if they consider their chances of eventual success to be low (Dweck 1986). Predictions of later performance based on value-added data may even encourage this negative effect. Feedback messages from assessment are very powerful, and it is important to ensure that the message emphasizes how to improve rather than failure to meet a standard.

One of the key features in the effective use of feedback is that it should encourage 'mindfulness' or conscious reflection on the part of the student, helping them to identify potential strategies (Bangert-Drowns, *et al.* 1991). As we suggested earlier, we consider mindfulness to be a learned characteristic that teachers should aim to develop through their feedback interactions. The quality of dialogue generated through feedback is significant for the development of mindfulness (Graesser, *et al.* 1995; Tanner and Jones 2000a). Unsurprisingly, there is evidence to suggest that oral feedback on students' work is the most effective in modifying learning behaviour (James 1998, p. 99). However, for practical reasons much of your feedback on their work is likely to be written and you should consider what forms of written feedback are likely to be most effective.

In most subject areas, children produce significant quantities of written work. Policy documents exist in most schools and departments that offer guidance about the frequency of marking that is expected and the form which marking should take, often including guidance on the way that work should be graded. Advice on the form that marking and grading should take varies widely from school to school, and often from department to department. Common practices include:

- an emphasis on mark schemes and grading, giving marks like 7/10, letter grades or National Curriculum (NC) levels;

- emotional or ego support through the use of smiley faces, ink stamps saying 'Ms Jones has seen this work' or supportive comments such as 'Good work!';

- general comments related to the task such as 'You are too untidy';

- specific instructions or targets for improvement such as: 'Show your working out'; 'Label your diagrams', or 'Try to explain why she was so sad';

- correction of errors, e.g. in calculation, spelling or method, showing the correct version alongside;

- an indication that a problem needs to be discussed, e.g. 'See me about this exercise during the lesson'. (Tanner and Jones 2003c, p. 64).

Some of these strategies support learning. Others are at best of dubious value, while others may even have a negative impact. We suggest that you pause to reflect on these strategies and others used in your own institution, analysing their potential to support the learning process before reading on.

Marking has sometimes been criticized for failing to indicate performance against external standards (Ofsted 2003). In response, some schools demand that work is graded against external examination or National Curriculum standards in order to provide meaning to the grades offered and achieve a degree of consistency between staff and focus children's attention on their performance in examinations. Unfortunately, such systems suffer from the problems of motivation described above. An emphasis on external standards also tends to focus the attention of students on performance rather than the learning process, with negative consequences.

The grading function of marking is often overemphasized at the expense of offering advice on how to learn more effectively. There is also a tendency for teachers to apply a normative approach to their marking, comparing students with each other and emphasizing competition rather than personal learning and development. Unfortunately, the research evidence suggests that the effect of such feedback practices is to convince weaker students that they lack ability, damaging their confidence in their ability to learn and de-motivating them. (Black and Wiliam 1998a).

Even when grades or marks are supplemented by comments, students seem to take little notice of the comments. Many comments take the form of emotional support like 'Good work!' or instructions about layout such as 'Use a ruler!' offering little in the way of substantial advice. Ofsted (2003) report that marking often fails to give sufficient guidance to students about how to improve their work, and that few opportunities are provided for students to reflect on their comments.

Advice and guidance on the best forms of feedback has been heavily influenced by the work of Butler (1987; 1988). This research distinguished between forms of feedback that focused on ego support and forms that focused on the demands of the task.

In the first study (Butler 1987), 200 5th and 6th Grade (Year 6 and Year 7) students in Israel were given divergent thinking tasks over three lessons and were given different forms of feedback at the start of the second lesson. One quarter was given individual comments, one quarter was given numerical grades, one quarter was given standardized praise and one quarter was given no feedback at all. The quality of the work of the groups was compared at the end of the third session. The quality of the work of those given comments had improved substantially. The work of those given praise or grades had failed to progress and achieved results equivalent to those of the control group who had received no feedback.

After the second lesson, students were given a questionnaire to establish whether they attributed their success to themselves (ego involvement) or the work they were doing (task involvement). Students who had received comments exhibited high levels of task involvement and exhibited no more ego involvement than the control group. Those given praise or grades had similar task involvement to the control group but higher ego involvement.

Students with high ego involvement tend to focus on their performance in relation to others and attribute their success or failure to their natural ability compared with others. Students with high-task involvement tend to focus on their interest in the subject and improving their performance. They tend to attribute their success or failure to effort and previous learning. High-task involvement is associated with improvements in performance. Praise and grades increase ego involvement without improving performance. In fact, lower performing students who attribute their failure to lack of ability are likely to become de-motivated and give up.

The second study (Butler 1988) involved 132 5th and 6th Grade (Year 6 and Year 7) students of high and low school achievement drawn from twelve classes in Israel. A mixture of convergent and divergent thinking tasks were attempted over three lessons. A pre-test was set at the start and classes were assessed at the end of the second lesson and without warning at the end of the third session. Feedback was given before the start of the second lesson. The twelve classes were randomly allocated to three feedback strategies: grades only, grades and comments, and comments only.

Students who received feedback through comments only performed significantly better than those who had received grades or grades and comments. They also showed significantly higher levels of interest. This applied to students classed as low achievement as well as those classed as high achievement. Students receiving either grades, or grades and comments made no progress. Those who received high marks showed high interest, and those who received low marks lost interest.

The implications for practice are clear. Our feedback should focus on task involvement rather than on ego involvement. We should focus on task-related comments, indicating to individual students what they need to improve and how to improve it. We should avoid the use of grades to compare students with each other, such as rank orders in class. Praise is not necessarily always a good thing. The quality of praise is more important than the quantity. Praise is most effective if it is infrequent, specific and genuine. Most importantly it should relate to something which is within the control of the student, such as the way they are approaching a learning task rather than some assumed innate ability (Good and Grouws 1975; Brophy 1981; Wiliam 1999b).

However, Butler's research (1987; 1988) is limited in several ways, being based on a theoretical experiment in an inauthentic setting. The size of sample is relatively small. The duration of the experiments is limited to three lessons in each case. The tasks were not drawn from the usual curriculum and the lessons were taught by psychology students in Israel. It is perhaps surprising that the results have been so influential on recent policy in the UK.

'Comments not grades' was one of the 102 strategies mentioned in individual action plans by the 24 teachers in the Kings Medway and Oxfordshire Formative Assessment Project (KMOFAP), which ran from January 1999 to July 2001. The project was based on local design – a form of action research – with teachers deciding for themselves which of a range of strategies to use to develop their use of formative assessment. Overall, the project demonstrated a strong positive effect, but the local design and multiple strategies employed made it impossible to isolate the impact of the 'comments not grades' strategy (Black, *et al.* 2003).

More recently, a year long project involving 104 Year 7 students in one South Wales comprehensive school resulted in a negative result (Smith and Gorad 2005). One mixed-ability class was given feedback in the form of comments only, while the remaining three parallel mixed-ability classes continued with the school policy of giving marks and grades with minimal associated comments. Value-added analyses based on standardized tests were used to compare the end of year internal assessment results of the groups in the core subjects. In English, Welsh and mathematics the control group outperformed the 'comment only' group. In Science no advantage was found for either group.

Interviews in the 'comments only' class revealed disquiet amongst many of the students, who felt at a disadvantage in not receiving marks like the other classes in their year. Several students expressed frustration at not being able to communicate their progress to their parents. Although the purpose of the project had been explained to them at the start of the year, many seemed confused about its purposes (Smith and Gorad 2005).

There are often problems when theoretical research or a project developed by enthusiasts is rolled out into wider practice. The teachers in the KMOFAP schools received significant training and support to ensure that they understood the principles underpinning the interventions. This was not the case in the Smith and Gorad project. In fact, some of the student interviews mention teachers giving out marks 'by mistake' and their receiving of National Curriculum levels.

Teachers described students as 'gagging for their marks' and students reported adding up their own ticks to work out their marks (Smith and Gorad 2005, p. 33–4). It would seem that a summative assessment culture still dominated amongst the students.

Furthermore, the nature of the comments used may have left much to be desired. The students report that comments were often of a form that would have been used alongside marks in the past, such as:

- 'try harder next time';

- 'very good';

- 'try and improve'.

To be formative, feedback should indicate what is wrong with the work and what needs to be done to improve. Advice needs to be precise, indicating the possible steps to be taken (Black, *et al.* 2003). This does not necessarily mean offering a complete, perfect solution. It is often better to discuss the nature of a perfect answer with the whole class but offer individual advice on written work that indicates a direction to follow, for example:

- Try to think of a more interesting ending for this story.

- Try adding these two equations.

- Why do you think Julius Caesar did this?

Such feedback demands an improved response from the student. For maximum impact, the student must attempt to follow the advice. The feedback is not a summative end-point, but a start-ing point for future learning. To be effective, time must be offered when work is returned for students to read the comments and try to act on them – perhaps ten minutes of reflection and response at the start of a lesson (Clarke 2005).

Such feedback is inevitably time consuming and is only man-ageable if other less-productive forms of assessment are no longer done by the teacher. Not all work can be marked in detail; when planning for formative assessment, teachers have to decide which aspects of their students' work needs to be should be marked in depth and which can be dealt with in other ways. Marking which merely indicates whether an answer is right or wrong fails to guide the student's further study and so might be more appropriate for student rather than teacher marking.

Marking a limited number of indicative pieces of work thoroughly, with detailed formative comments that must be responded to, will contribute far more to the student's learning than marking a large volume superficially. Unfortunately, school and departmental assessment policies often focus teachers' marking strategies on summative functions, leaving them with little time for meaningful formative comments.

Students need to learn how to ask for help and deal with helpful advice, and the ethos of the school should encourage them to do so (QCA 2001a, b). Feedback which invites the opening of a dialogue, like 'See me at the end of the lesson to discuss this', may encourage them in this, but only if they are encultured to view it as an offer of learning support rather than an implied criticism and punishment. A classroom culture must be developed that encourages children to believe that to make mistakes is a natural part of the learning process. A wrong or incomplete answer should be seen as an opportunity to learn, rather than a cause for teacher displeasure. Criticism of an incorrect approach or misconception must be dissociated from criticism of the child.

Success was unlikely in Smith and Gorad's (2005) intervention, without a root and branch change in school culture. A change in one aspect of assessment policy does not by itself effect a cultural change. Developing a formative assessment culture in a school requires far more than the bolt-on application of a few simple strategies or 'tips for teachers'. What is demanded is a re-evaluation of the pedagogical contract between teachers and students and the development of a culture in which the learner and the teacher are in a collaborative relationship based on the processes of learning rather than the imposition of external standards. The development of a formative assessment culture is a complex change and, in common with most ideas of worth, requires in-depth understanding of the nature and purposes of the change, and the development of skill and commitment to make it work (Fullan 1993, p. 22–3).

## Attitudes to assessment and learning

Developing an effective formative assessment culture demands a change to the traditional dialogue between teachers and students. Although we use the phrase formative assessment, Barnes (1976) prefers to distinguish between summatively assessing students' oral or written thoughts, and replying to them. When replying to students, teachers are taking students' views seriously, even if they intend to challenge, extend or modify them. In traditional forms of assessment, the teachers tend to focus on external standards and, by implication, devalue the constructions of the learner. Both assessing and replying are necessary parts of teaching – clearly there are times when relating children's knowledge to externally imposed standards is appropriate: it is the balance that is the issue.

> If a teacher stresses the assessment function at the expense of the reply function, this will urge his students towards externally acceptable performances rather than towards trying to relate new knowledge to old. (Barnes 1976, p. 111).

Unfortunately, the language of accountability and standards has dominated official guidance since the early 1990s and the culture prevailing in many schools has become distorted in ways which have become so 'taken for granted' that we hardly notice their impact.

In a summative assessment culture, when work is returned to students, they have two over-riding concerns: What was my mark? Did I do better or worse than my friends? They are often encouraged in this by the treatment of marks as something substantial that have been gained, rather than indicators of learning. In such a culture, few students attempt to use the results of assessment formatively. They regard their results as 'summary indicators of their success; they do not see them as serving their interests and do not look for feedback about how to improve the way that they work' (Black 1998a, p. 135). In fact, most students regard the regular summative assessments they endure as being for the benefit of the school or their parents, rather than for themselves. Assessment is seen as something that is intended to make them work harder rather than differently (Black, 1998b, p. 43). This attitude is a major obstacle to progress.

In order to take full advantage of the proven benefits of formative assessment, school culture should encourage students to take control of their own learning and responsibility for their own progress. The extent to which students are able to take control of their own learning and use the information which is provided to them from formative assessment, is conditional on their beliefs about the causes of success and failure. When school culture tends to support the view that ability is fixed and unchangeable, students are unlikely to take advantage of the positive messages that are contained in feedback.

Three factors are generally considered to govern attributions of success or failure. First, the extent to which you judge your performance to be determined by internal or external factors. For example, did I get a good mark because it was a good piece of work or because I had an easy marker? Second, whether your success or failure is due to stable or unstable factors. For example, did I get a bad examination result because I lack ability (out of my control) or did I get a bad examination result because I was unlucky (out of my control) or did no revision (within my control)? Third, I'm good/bad at that, but that's the only thing I'm good/bad at, versus I'm good/bad at that, therefore I'm good/bad at everything (Wiliam 1999b, p. 10).

In the end, what matters is whether students and their teachers view ability as fixed or incremental. If the school culture supports the view that ability is incremental or trainable, then challenges are more likely to be seen as opportunities to learn. Formative assessment should be presented as an opportunity to learn and improve rather than as a threatening situation in which self-esteem might be lost (Wiliam 1999b, p. 10).

On the other hand, in more traditional cultures that regard ability as fixed and unchangeable, students are likely to view every assessment event as an opportunity to either re-affirm their ability or be shown up. Current high-attainers, who are confident in their ability to succeed, tend to accept the challenge, whereas many other students (particularly boys) would prefer to be thought of as lazy and uncommitted rather than dumb, and seek to bolster their self-respect in other ways.

For formative assessment to achieve its true potential in enhancing learning, our students must have attitudes and beliefs that encourage them to use feedback positively. Some students are already able to use assessment information positively to improve their performance in summative assessments (Brookhart 2001). This minority of more successful students have learned how to use assessment data to help them learn. They have taken control of their own learning and are able to assess their knowledge, identify areas for development and set themselves targets for their own learning. In the end, the main aim of formative assessment must be to enable students to take control of their own destinies. They must learn how to learn and assess themselves if they are to become lifelong learners who are independent of the advice of their teachers.

# 4

# Self-assessment and learning to learn

Much of the focus of the book so far has been on the teacher's role in developing the productive use of assessment for learning. But, unlike traditional assessment procedures, assessment for learning is not a spectator sport. Assessment for learning is not something that is done to students, but a process that is undertaken in collaboration with them. If assessment is to have maximum impact on the learning process, then students must be active participants.

## Involving students in their own assessment

Why should students be involved in their own assessment? One rather pragmatic reason is that of efficiency – teachers can't mark everything! If you wish to have the time to comment constructively on students' work, offering quality feedback, then you have to be selective in what you mark. Students have to learn how to take responsibility for assessing the remaining aspects of their work. They also have to learn how to learn from this process.

It is difficult to manage your own learning without being able to assess yourself – if you do not know what you already know then it is difficult to decide what to learn next. Students need to be able to assess themselves, to identify their strengths and weaknesses. They have to be able to set themselves targets for improvement, and they have to learn how to use a variety of resources to help them with this. While reference to external standards such as National Curriculum levels has a place, day-to-day assessment for learning has to be far more fine-grained and personal in nature if it is to be useful.

The prevalence of high-stakes summative assessments has led to far too many students believing that the important outcome from an activity is their mark rather than their learning. Their focus should be modified to developing strategies for learning rather than acquiring marks. Their role should be to analyse their current knowledge to identify their learning needs and plan their next steps. Involving students in assessment develops a learning culture within the class whereby students come to realize that the purpose of the lesson is for them to learn rather than for the teacher to teach. Involving students in their own assessment gives them ownership of and responsibility for their own learning.

In other words, the main reason for involving students in their own assessment is to help them to become independent, lifelong learners. After all, they will not always have the teacher with them to highlight errors or to suggest improvements. Students have to develop the ability to do such things for themselves. We compare this to dependence on a calculator – you need mental methods for all those times when you don't have the calculator to hand!

As we discussed in the last chapter, the nature of the feedback from assessment can enhance the learning process and facilitate the development of self-regulated learning. In this chapter we explore how active involvement in peer- and self-assessment may help students learn how to learn.

For students to be able to use assessment formatively to enhance their own learning, the feedback must help them to:

- develop their understanding of themselves as learners;
- be clear about what they understand and what they are unsure about – they must know what they know already;
- know what they are trying to achieve;

- choose a strategy to help them to build on what they know;

- have the motivation to learn. (Sadler 1989; Black and Wiliam 1998a; Tanner, *et al.* 2002)

These factors are metacognitive in character. Metacognition refers to your knowledge and beliefs about what you know and your skills for controlling your thinking (Flavell 1976, p. 232). Metacognition has three elements: metacognitive knowledge, metacognitive beliefs and self-regulation skills (Flavell 1976; Tanner and Jones 1994; 1995; 1999; 2000a).

Metacognitive knowledge, or knowing what you know, includes the awareness you have of your own knowledge, your strengths and weaknesses. Such self-knowledge is necessary for effective and efficient learning. Metacognitive beliefs also include your beliefs about yourself as a learner; how you think you learn best and how likely you are to succeed in learning a subject. Such beliefs strongly influence your motivation to learn. You also have metacognitive knowledge and beliefs about the nature of the subject you are learning, that is, what you perceive to be important in a subject and hence what the nature of a good answer would be. For example, if you think that learning science is really about memorizing facts and collecting marks, then what is important about your answer is that it should be marked as correct. Understanding scientific process and the evidence base would not appear to be relevant. Such beliefs influence what you expect to learn in a subject and what learning strategies you are prepared to employ.

If your focus is just on getting the right answer, then looking up the answer in the back of the book would be cheating. If, however, you look up the answer, use it to identify the thinking that led to it or where you went wrong and then complete the task successfully, then that is a sensible and valid learning strategy for overcoming a difficulty. Similarly, discussing work with a friend is only cheating if, at the end of the conversation, the answer is copied in without understanding it or recreating it for yourself. We have seen many classrooms posters about cheating that suggest that in the end you are cheating if you pretend to understand when you don't, and then you are cheating yourself. Students' metacognitive beliefs affect and are affected by the learning culture within the classroom.

Metacognitive skills refer to the strategies used to monitor and control the learning process. They involve the making and monitoring of your own choices. This includes your ability to set targets for what you want to learn next, your awareness of possible strategies for learning this, the choice of strategy, planning your learning, monitoring your progress and evaluating whether your learning goals have been achieved.

Metacognition is closely related to self-directed learning and conceptual development, and research shows that improving metacognition improves learning (Brown 1987; Tanner 1997). The interaction between knowing what you know already, what strategies you have to overcome, your weaknesses, and your beliefs about yourself as a learner of a subject all significantly affect the effectiveness of your learning.

Low-achieving students tend to have poor metacognitive knowledge and skills. Fortunately, research has demonstrated that teaching strategies focused on improving metacognition lead to more effective learning (Cardelle-Elawar 1992, 1995; Tanner 1997). Engaging in formative self-assessment is likely to support the development of metacognitive skills, which are likely to help students to develop into more effective learners in other areas (Black 1998a, p. 133).

Unfortunately, the use of self-assessment is not common. The LEARN project found that fewer than 25 per cent of GCSE, GNVQ and A-level students had opportunities to assess their own work, and that of the self-assessment that did occur, most was limited to self-marking or use of answers at the back of the textbook (CLIO 2000, p. 4). Although some students may choose to reflect on which questions they got wrong and why, most just tick or cross unthinkingly. Self-marking saves teacher time but has little impact on learning unless the reasons for errors are probed. Such a restricted interpretation of self-assessment does not provide students with formative feedback, nor does it highlight what is considered to be important within the task. For assessment to improve learning, students need to be involved in more pro-found ways.

One reason why self-assessment is not common might be that its use is not straightforward. Whatever task we set for students usually has two aims: we expect students to achieve both the object of the task (for example, making an artefact, finding answers to questions) and also to learn from the attempt. To achieve the object of the task requires an understanding of the criteria for a good performance, but to learn from the task requires a sense of their own learning (Blanchard 1993, p. 37). For self-assessment to improve students' learning it must develop their understanding of the assessment criteria and encourage them to become self-monitoring and reflective (Brooks 2002, p. 69).

Many students lack a clear overview of their own learning and become confused because they do not understand the criteria against which they are being assessed (QCA 2001b, p. 5). This is particularly true when open-ended coursework tasks are used as part of the examination process. For self-assessment to be successful, students must understand the assessment criteria and have internalized the general characteristics to the extent that they can interpret them within a particular context. In the Practical Applications of Mathematics Project (PAMP), we found that many students were unable to do this (Tanner and Jones 1994; 1995; 2000a, b). Similarly, attempts to introduce self-assessment into the Standard Assessment Tasks (SATs) were unsuccessful – students lacked the necessary skills for self-assessment. Research suggests that when students are first intro-duced to self-assessment they find it difficult, and that they need to be taught how to assess themselves (Tanner and Jones 1994; Black 1998a, pp. 128–35).

> For formative assessment to be productive, pupils should be trained in self-assessment so that they can understand the main purposes of their learning and thereby grasp what they need to do to achieve. (Black and Wiliam 1998b, p. 10).

We need to add a note of caution here: involving students in their own assessment requires more than just helping them to identify what they need to do to 'close the gap'. Learning should involve more than attempting to meet examination assessment criteria or achieve the teacher's lesson objectives. Successful students continually self-assess their understanding for internal consistency and look for situations where their learning could be applied (Brookhart 2001).

Research suggests that involving students in self-assessment can lead to very large learning gains (Tanner and Jones 1995, 1999, 2000a, 2003a; Black and Wiliam 1998a; Black, *et al.* 2003). The PAMP and the KMOFAP projects, which we discussed earlier, indicated the large gains that could be made by secondary students in the areas of mathematics and science. Similar gains are reported elsewhere. The introduction of frequent, regular student self-assessment activities over an eight-month period by 25 teachers of Year 3/4 students in Portugal resulted in significant gains in mathematics – almost double those of the matched control classes. As part of the self-assessment activities, students were encouraged to set their own learning goals, to plan and carry out learning tasks to achieve these goals and to evaluate their own learning (Fernandes and Fontana 1996, p. 304). Other smaller studies have also reported that the introduction of self-assessment activities, which led students to reflect on their learning strategies, resulted in positive gains in students' learning: for example, of Year 7 students' knowledge of spelling and punctuation (Lee and Gavine 2003) and of Grade 3 students' knowledge of multiplication facts

(Brookhart, *et al.* 2004). More importantly, such activities resulted in the development of students' metacognition.

One of the features of the projects which led to significant and sustained improvements in students' learning was the involvement of teachers in professional development and discussion of pedagogy; the teachers were helped to:

> . . . modify the classroom environment in order to strengthen the effect of pupil self-assessment strategies and did not teach the techniques concerned in a mechanical and a-critical way. (Fernandes and Fontana 1996, p. 311).

Effective use of peer- and self-assessment requires more than just a bolt-on approach; it has to become an integral part of the learning culture in the classroom, and students need to be taught how to engage with such techniques.

## Developing peer- and self-assessment

The successful projects included both peer- and self-assessment and a variety of teaching approaches. However, we would argue that learning to assess the work of others through peer-assessment is a developmental first step in learning how to assess yourself (cf. Jones 1992; Tanner and Jones 1994; Black, *et al.* 2003). Furthermore, we suggest that you start by whole-class assessment of an anonymous piece of work. There are a number of reasons for this:

- it allows you to establish 'ground rules' before students comment on the work of their classmates;

- you can model how you assess and how to make a constructive response;

- it allows you to intervene to guide student discussion of what they perceive to be important features;

65

- it helps to clarify for students what are the good features of a piece of work;

- it starts to develop a classroom culture of reflecting constructively on a piece of work;

- it increases student ownership of the assessment process.

The process of self-assessment demands that students compare their work against some form of quality criteria. If the work is associated with external examination, for example, as in a coursework task, then a major issue may be interpreting general examination criteria in the context of a particular task. Otherwise, the generation and internalization of assessment criteria contributes to the development of an understanding of what is valued within a particular subject discipline. This is not trivial; it is learning to think like a mathematician, scientist, historian, etc. – becoming encultured to the subject.

We sometimes start the process by preparing an 'exemplar' piece of work which contains features that we wish to highlight. We ask the students to read the work for themselves and to compare it with assessment criteria which have been written in task-specific, student-friendly language. Students then discuss their assessments in small groups. Selected groups are then asked to present their assessments to the class and, during the subsequent discussion, the teacher intervenes to focus attention on key aspects and to clarify what is considered important and why. The discussion ends with each group proposing a constructive suggestion for improving the work still further. Once again, the teacher may intervene here to indicate what sorts of comments are acceptable and helpful.

An alternative approach is to start by asking students to discuss what criteria they would set for the task and then to brainstorm their suggestions. During the subsequent whole-class discussion, the teacher can focus attention on key features and lead the class towards an agreed set of criteria. This approach has the advantage of revealing to the teacher what students perceive to be important in their work.

In both approaches, the small-group discussions help students to begin to analyse and reflect on what they consider to be important in the task. The whole-class discussions generate a shared understanding of the criteria which can be moderated by teacher interventions.

The use of anonymous work in the first instance avoids embarrassment, as the teacher helps students learn how to make their comments constructive in nature: but there is additional value to the process when students learn to critique each other's work. For example, in a lesson we observed in the Raising Standards in Numeracy (RSN) project (Tanner, *et al.* 1999; 2002), three students were chosen to write their solutions to a homework problem on the whiteboard as a Year 10 mathematics class entered the room and settled down. By the time the students had settled, three different solutions were written out on the board. The solutions were then thrown open for discussion by the class and their authors challenged to explain their approaches. The authors and the class then engaged in self- and peer-assessment of the work, eventually judging how many marks would have been gained by each solution in a GCSE examination.

Mathematics might be thought to be particularly amenable to peer-assessment because of its apparently more objective nature; however, many examples of peer- and self-assessment come from the arts subjects (see, for example, Ross, *et al.* 1993; AifL 2005a, b). Identifying a good solution to a task requiring merely low-level factual knowledge or skills is straightforward – the answer is either correct or not. In contrast, the criteria for assessment of more complex domains, such as coursework tasks or the process attainment targets of the National Curriculum, tend to be expressed in rather general, abstract terms. Students need help to interpret such criteria within the context of a particular task. Peer-assessment enables the less concrete and more aesthetic aspects of students' work to be discussed, exemplified and internalized (Ross, *et al.* 1993).

For example, one KMOFAP teacher wished to improve her students' accents when speaking French. She gave out an extract of French text to small groups of students. Each member of the group had to read the piece in turn, and the student with the best accent was chosen to represent the group in a whole-class plenary. Each representative read the piece to the class and the teacher facilitated a whole-class discussion on which student had the best accent and why. Although it is not possible to define the features of a good accent precisely, all were helped to improve their own accents (Black, *et al.* 2003, p. 73).

One common strategy is the peer-marking of draft work. For example, as part of the LEARN project (CLIO 2000, p. 4), drafts of A-level English essays were peer-assessed and the comments used to rework them prior to submission.

Further, the 'traffic-light' system can be used to help students indicate areas for improvement, as shown to be effective in an AifL case study (2005a). Student-friendly versions of assessment criteria, set out in a mind map, were given to Standard 3 (Scottish equivalent to Year 10) students to peer-mark their critical appraisals of a poem. Working in pairs, students exchanged first drafts of their essays. They used the diagrams to give each other feedback by using colour-coding to indicate which criteria had been well done (circled in green), which were badly done (circled in red) and which could be improved (circled in amber). The annotated diagram then formed the basis for discussion and clarification between the marker and author, resulting in a clearer idea of how the second draft of the essay would be assessed.

As another example, in a Standard 1 (Scottish equivalent to Year 8) art class, students were given four specific criteria to focus their work on. They then swapped work with their partners and assessed it against the criteria using the traffic-light system.

If criteria were not green-lighted then the marker had to indicate why and explain how the work could be improved (AifL 2005b).

The use of peer-assessment develops an understanding of the assessment criteria for task. It also helps students to see their efforts in the light of the whole situation and against the means by which the quality of performance will be viewed, and to govern their efforts accordingly (Blanchard 1993, p. 37). If the work which has been redrafted following peer comments is then formally marked, the final grades may well be higher than would have been achieved unaided (Tanner and Jones 1994). However, such formative assessment is part of the teaching and learning process rather than a summative judgement, and its value lies in helping to indicate what a student is able to achieve if the advice given is acted upon and internalized.

Involvement in peer-assessment then is 'uniquely valuable' for several reasons:

- it motivates students to take pride in their work and present it more carefully;

- the shared language used in peer discussion may help to convince other students of the value and feasibility of the task;

- criticism from their peers may be more influential than from the teacher;

- feedback from groups strengthens the student voice and improves communication between teacher and students about their learning;

- it provides time for the teacher to observe and reflect on what is happening and to frame productive interventions (Summarized from Black, *et al.* 2003, pp. 50–1).

The success of such approaches rests on a number of factors, however. First, the students must believe that ability is not fixed but trainable; otherwise the discrepancy between particularly good work and their own may intimidate rather than inspire. Second, peer-assessment requires discussion between students and therefore the classroom ethos must facilitate supportive, open debate. Third, the feedback from the comments and discussions must provide scaffolding to improve learning. In particular, care must be taken to prevent students uncritically accepting work of a mediocre standard, or reinforcing each other's errors and misconceptions. This is where the teacher's interventions are crucial. As we discussed in Chapter 1, focusing questioning may provide dynamic scaffolding for students to test the validity of their ideas and to help them to work within their Zone of Proximal Development (ZPD).

Such peer-assessment strategies are helpful in generating a shared understanding of the assessment criteria and what is important in the task. During the discussions and activities, students may choose to reflect 'in action' (Schön 1990) on how these apply to their own work. However, more formal opportunities for 'reflection on action' are necessary to develop the metacognitive knowledge needed for self-assessment (c.f. Piaget 1977).

During the PAMP project (Tanner and Jones 1994), self-reflection was encouraged when students presented draft reports of their investigations to the class for peer-assessment. Students were encouraged to ask the presenters for explanation of any points which were unclear to them, but the ground rules were made clear and enforced – comments had to indicate strengths as well as weaknesses, and any criticism had to be accompanied by a justification and suggestions for improvement. Initially, much of the questioning was led by the teachers in order to focus attention on significant aspects of the report and to model the type of questioning expected. Certain generic questions were frequently used, for example, 'Will that always be true?', 'How can you be sure that . . .?' To encourage 'looking back' the teachers always asked: 'If you were to do this task again, what would you do differently?'

Gradually, students realized that such questions were always asked, and began to copy the teachers' style of question during the discussion. More importantly, however, it became clear that the students had internalized the types of questions and were asking themselves such questions as a framework to structure their work and to prepare their presentations. They had learned the metacognitive skills necessary to plan, monitor and evaluate their work and were, thereby, developing control over their own learning. They had begun to assess themselves, and such self-assessment results in genuine improvements in learning.

Asking students to report back on draft work, therefore, serves two purposes. Its apparent aim is to improve the final report through discussion and constructive criticism. However, the most effective teachers used the plenary to develop students' skills of peer- and self-assessment through engaging the class in collective reflection. Although the need to help students understand task criteria is most apparent in complex domains, many of the techniques discussed here can be used to teach more straightforward subject content knowledge.

In fact, in the second phase of the PAMP project, students who had engaged in collective reflection through peer- and self-assessment were found to perform significantly better than their matched control groups in aspects of mathematics which had not been targeted by the project (sig <0.1%, effect size 0.2, Tanner and Jones 2000a; 2003a). Their learning had not only been about 'Using and Applying Mathematics', they had learned to reflect on their learning and to assess themselves. They had learned how to learn and used their new thinking skills when learning other material. A similar effect is reported by the Cognitive Acceleration in Science Education (CASE) project, with improved performance found in non-science subjects as children learned to learn (Adey and Shayer 1993; Shayer and Adey 2002).

Collective reflection leads students to assess themselves, and develops their metacognitive self-knowledge. It can be facilitated in a variety of ways. Many of the successful teachers in the RSN project used reflective assessment activities in their lesson plenaries. These included asking students:

- to identify warnings which they would give to other students about to start the same task;

- to identify what is important for them to remember from today's lesson (Tanner and Jones 2000b, p. 204).

A particularly effective strategy was to give out work from an imaginary student that exemplified common misconceptions and errors. Small groups of students then discussed the work trying to understand the thinking that had led to the mistakes. Research suggests that addressing misconceptions directly in this way provides opportunities for effective learning (Askew and Wiliam 1995). Following class discussion, the task of writing help notes to the imaginary student was set for homework. Students enjoyed annotating the work with helpful comments that a teacher might have written. Pretending to act as a teacher for another student enabled them to stand back from the topic and reflect on the learning process. Explaining a concept to another person deepens your own understanding, as most of us discovered when we first began teaching.

Such activities require students to articulate what they have learned and what they found difficult. This requires them to reflect back on their own learning. It also provides formative feedback to the teacher on what the students perceived the lesson objectives to have been. Telling students the learning objectives does not guarantee that they will understand or accept them!

Similar approaches include appointing a student to act as a 'rapporteur' during the plenary to summarize the main points of the lesson and to answer any questions from other students (Wiliam 2000). This may appear to be a very threatening activity, but in the PAMP and RSN projects we found students willingly volunteered to take the 'hot seat'. They perceived such activities to be productive opportunities to test out their understanding and to identify aspects for improvement. The classroom climate supported open, collaborative enquiry in which mistakes were expected and seen as learning opportunities.

Acting as a rapporteur requires you to test yourself against the questioning of others, but part of developing your metacognitive knowledge is to know which aspects of the work are most problematic for you. Some RSN teachers regularly asked students to write their own test questions at the end of a topic (Tanner, *et al.* 1999).

Writing a good question to assess a student's knowledge of a topic requires a deeper understanding of the subject, including recognizing structural features and an insight into what might make a question difficult or even impossible to answer. You probably began to realize this when you first started teaching and discovered that writing questions for other people deepened your knowledge of your subject. Consider these examples on ratio:

A    Divide £20 in the ratio 3:2

B    Divide £20 in the ratio 4:3

C    Two girls divided a sum of money in the ratio 2:3.
       The first girl got £8. How much did the second girl get?

A is a relatively straightforward question because 3 and 2 add to make 5 and 5 divides into 20 exactly. In question B on the other hand 4 plus 3 makes 7, and 7 does not divide into 20 exactly. To understand why B is harder than A requires a deeper understanding of ratio than is required to answer straightforward textbook examples that have been chosen to work out easily. Example C demands that the student recognize underlying structural features in the mathematics in order to be able to answer a question in a slightly unusual format.

73

Groups of students tried out each other's questions then chose the 'best' one to present to the whole class. The ensuing discussion focused on which questions were 'good'. Features of good questions were considered to include those which required key knowledge or skills, tested common difficulties or misconceptions, were set in unusual contexts or phrased differently. Students took pride in writing the hardest, most unusual questions they could, with the incentive that one of the 'best' questions would, in fact, be included in the end-of-module test. The range of questions attempted also generated a good set of revision notes for the class (this is discussed further in Chapter 5). More importantly, such activities require students to reflect on their own learning, to develop their metacognitive knowledge and to identify suitable aspects for improvement. The calibre of the questions and the discussion also provide feedback to the teacher about students' perceptions of what is important in their learning and their level of understanding (Tanner, *et al.* 2002).

More formal written feedback about the extent of students' understanding may also be generated through self-assessment activities. Students' perceptions of the extent to which they have understood each of the lesson objectives may be gathered by asking them to indicate this at the end of the lesson, perhaps by using tick boxes or sad/smiley faces (Wiliam 2000). This strategy has the advantage of providing the teacher with a written record of the students' perceptions of their understanding and helps to indicate areas of work which need review.

Self-evaluation of students' degree of understanding of key concepts is also useful in preparation for or as a response to more formal assessment tasks. QCA (2001b) reports on a school using 'traffic light' self-assessment when reviewing half-term tests. Students maintained their own record-of-attainment sheets on which they indicated the extent to which they felt they had understood the learning objectives associated with particular questions. A green blob meant 'I understood this and feel confident'. A green blob could be used next to an incorrect answer if the error was trivial. An amber blob indicated that they had some understanding but were not confident, feeling 'not sure' about the topic. This might be used even if the question was correct in the test. A red blob meant 'I don't understand at all'.

Some teachers follow up traffic light self-assessments with a peer-support session in which students with green blobs help students with amber blobs to correct work where necessary, allowing the teacher to focus on the students with red blobs. Some of the RSN teachers used such a system prior to the assessment, setting probing revision questions on a topic for the 'green and amber' students to work through in pairs, while they worked with the 'reds' (see also KMOFAP in Black, *et al.* 2003).

The annotated record-of-attainment sheets provided a cumulative, written record of students' ongoing progress. Such records are fine-grained but manageable, as the responsibility for maintaining them rests with the students. The information recorded provides a useful basis for discussion and target-setting in a progress review or at a parents' evening. Placing the responsibility for recording on the student allows teachers to spend more time analysing areas of strength and weakness, discussing misconceptions and helping students to plan their learning.

In a very strong summative assessment culture, you may be concerned that the reliability of self-assessment is suspect and that students might be over-confident or even cheat. However, we feel that this misses the point. In formative self-assessment it is validity rather than reliability which is important. The aim of self-assessment is to improve learning and not to allocate grades and this must be communicated to students. Most studies into self-assessment report that, when properly prepared, students have generally been found to be honest and accurate when assessing their own work and that of their peers (such as Freeman and Lewis 1998).

The variety of peer- and self-assessment approaches discussed above all contribute towards a clearer understanding of learning objectives and assessment criteria through the articulation of students' tentative ideas and reflection on their own learning. Involving students in their own assessment seeks to develop their metacognitive knowledge of their strengths and weaknesses, and their understanding of the learning objectives they are being asked to achieve. It aims to develop their metacognitive skills so that they can plan, monitor and evaluate their own learning strategies. Most importantly, it is intended to influence students' beliefs about themselves as learners – to convince them that they are able to improve their performance through their own efforts, and to motivate them to take control of their own learning.

## The importance of reflection and metacognition in self-regulated learning

Assessment often has an emotional as well as a cognitive impact. Insensitive feedback can damage motivation, and some students learn from quite an early age that they are losers in the educational race and that there is little point in trying. Sylva (1994) describes the early emergence of two types of learner: the mastery child and the helpless child. Mastery children:

- are motivated by the desire to learn;

- will tackle difficult tasks in flexible and reflective ways;

- are confident of success, believing they can do it if they try;

- believe that you can improve your intelligence;

- if they see another hard-working child, they will say 'she must be interested'.

In contrast, helpless children:

- are motivated by a desire to be seen to do well;
- seem to accept that they will fail because they are just not clever enough;
- believe that if something seems too hard there is nothing they can do about it;
- tend therefore to avoid any challenge;
- do not believe that they can improve their intelligence (Sylva 1994 cited in Black 1998a, pp. 133–4).

However, regular use of self-assessment strategies have been shown to lead to increased academic competence and feelings of personal control which, in turn, lead to increased motivation to learn (Fernandes and Fontana 1996, p. 304). Lee and Gavine (2003) found that as students became used to reflecting on their learning there was an increase in the use of more metacognitive strategies, such as reviewing their work or reading more slowly, which were under the control of the students, and a decrease in their attributions of performance to external, uncontrollable factors.

The learning behaviour of students is dependent on a complex interaction between a number of factors, including their interest in the subject, their desire to succeed at school, the learning strategies they have experienced or been taught, and their beliefs about themselves as learners. Particularly critical are their judgements about their potential to learn. These factors are gathered together in the concept of self-efficacy (Bandura 1977). Children's self-efficacy is dependent on the quality of assessment they have received over the years and the extent to which feedback messages have led them to perceive themselves as successful or unsuccessful learners.

Students' self-efficacy for a subject may be defined as their judgements about their potential to learn the subject successfully.

Students with higher levels of self-efficacy set higher goals, apply more effort, persist longer in the face of difficulty and are more likely to use self-regulated learning strategies (Bandura 1977; Wolters and Rosenthal 2000).

The development of autonomous, self-regulated, lifelong learners depends on the interaction of three linked psychological domains of functioning: the affective, the cognitive and the conative (Bandura, 1977).

The affective domain includes students' beliefs about themselves and their capacity to learn; the extent to which they attribute success or failure to innate or controllable factors; their perceived status as learners; their beliefs about the nature of understanding; and their potential to succeed in the subject.

The cognitive domain includes the students' awareness of their own knowledge of the subject: their knowledge of their strengths and weaknesses; the general principles they are able to articulate; the specific strategies they know they can use in particular contexts; and their development of links between aspects of the subject (Tanner and Jones, 2003a, b).

Whilst these two domains represent highly significant aspects of metacognition, the principal value of self-efficacy for improving learning rests in the third domain. The conative domain links the affective and cognitive domains to pro-active (as opposed to reactive or habitual) behaviour. It relates to the inclination to strive and the strategies that they employ in support of their learning. It includes their disposition to plan, monitor and evaluate their work and their inclination to mindfulness and reflection. In particular, it includes the strategies that they are inclined to use when reviewing or revising their work (Snow 1996).

Only a minority of students are motivated to learn by high-stakes summative assessment. In fact, most students (and their teachers) tend to focus on test performance rather than understanding. There is a tendency for extrinsic motivation to be over-emphasized at the expense of intrinsic. This often leads to shallow, rather than deep, learning and a reduction in self-efficacy and effort for a significant proportion of students (Harlen and Deakin Crick 2002).

Unfortunately, the political pressures on schools to use intermittent summative assessments of students' learning are unlikely to reduce in the near future. However, many of the negative effects we have described can be ameliorated if the learning culture in the school emphasizes formative rather than summative functions. There is evidence that the most successful students know how to use intermittent summative assessment formatively to support their own self-regulated learning (Brookhart 2001). The issue is to develop a school culture that regards examinations as a starting point in the learning process, rather than an end point.

# 5

# Using examinations to support learning

## High-stakes examinations versus formative assessment

The focus of this book so far has been on the development of a formative assessment culture in your school or department in order to improve learning. While doing this we have drawn attention to the uneasy tension that exists between the formative and the summative functions of assessment. We suggest that many of the criticisms of current assessment practices made by the Assessment Reform Group (ARG) and others are related to an overemphasis on the summative and managerial functions of assessment at the expense of formative functions, and our intention has been to encourage you to redress that balance (Black and Wiliam 1998a; ARG 2002; Tanner and Jones 2003c).

In so doing we do not reject the value of the summative functions of assessment. We recognize the need for learners to pause to reflect on their overall progress at intervals, to draw together knowledge from a variety of topics, to make links and review their learning. Such assessment information is likely to be demanded by managers at various levels within the education system for purposes of accountability, communication and selection. It is clear that, for the foreseeable future, formative assessment will have to co-exist alongside high-stakes summative assessments, such as examinations.

Some of the advantages claimed for examinations are that:

- they set and demand standards;
- they exemplify to pupils what must be learned;

- rewards and penalties can be applied to results;

- they motivate children to learn. (Kellaghan, *et al.* 1996)

However, there is evidence that not all children are equally motivated by high-stakes examinations, with many low-attaining students actually de-motivated by a regime in which they believe themselves to be inevitable losers and in which they often have no effective strategies for change (Black and Wiliam 1998a, b; Harlen and Deakin Crick 2002).

Furthermore, many of the apparent gains that are attributed to examinations are actually the result of teachers learning how to teach to the test, and training students how to maximize their scores rather than their learning (Kohn 2000). Even when examinations are designed to assess higher order thinking, such aims may be subverted by teachers and learners who focus on performance rather than process or learning goals (Kellaghan, *et al.* 1996; Gordon and Rees 1997).

When performance in high-stakes summative assessment is allowed to become the main goal of education rather than an indicator of learning, the backwash effect on teaching and learning styles is often negative, with short-term instrumental learning driving out the search for understanding and longer-term educational goals. In such circumstances, evidence suggests that teachers and students make little use of the formative functions of assessment to support learning. One major backwash effect of high-stakes summative assessment can be to squeeze out formative assessment (Harlen and Deakin-Crick 2002).

However, the effect on children and their learning is not uniform. Research with high-attaining students suggests that they tend to use self-assessment and self-monitoring on a regular basis. They know how to deal with feedback in whatever form it is offered and, in particular, they are able to make formative use of summative assessment (Sadler 1989, 1998; Brookhart 2001). The highest attaining students know how to learn and how to use the feedback from examinations to further their learning. More than this, their whole outlook on learning involves a natural searching for the formative (Brookhart 2001).

Achievers learn how to achieve, and using assessment information formatively is a big part of that process. (Brookhart 2001, p.166).

However, this is far more than good examination technique or learning for the test. It is not as concrete or mechanical as suggested by the much-quoted metaphor of 'closing the gap' between their current position and a given standard (Sadler 1989; QCA 2001a). Their focus is on learning rather than performance. Their targets are more complex than the passing of an examination, and include a view of learning as an important life-long process (Brookhart 2001).

Can you help the ordinary student to learn the successful strategies employed by the high-attainers and develop the attitudes that will help them to become successful lifelong learners? Much depends on the development of a formative assessment culture within your school or classroom, based on learning rather than performance. Summative assessment does not have to squeeze out formative assessment. This is where the concept of *assessment event* is helpful. The issue is not the form of the examination itself, but the nature of the preparation beforehand, involving note-taking, review and revision, and the analysis, reflection and personal target-setting that occur afterwards. The way teachers present and encourage such activities contributes significantly to the development of a formative assessment culture, particularly if children are actively taught appropriate strategies and guided through processes that lead them to develop skills of self-assessment and self-regulation.

If such activities are to contribute to an effective learning culture around examinations, as opposed to a performance culture, a number of conditions must be met. First, the students' self-efficacy must be high. They must believe that their ability is not fixed but trainable. Second, they must have metacognitive knowledge of their own strengths and weaknesses. Third, they must be aware of, and be inclined to use, effective strategies for reviewing and revising their work and analysing their strengths and weaknesses. Fourth, after an examination they must be inclined to analyse their answers in the light of feedback and be able to identify areas for development, using targeted learning strategies to turn today's failure into tomorrow's success.

Self-efficacy is often low amongst low-attaining and even middle-of-the-road students (Tanner and Jones 2003b). Furthermore, school culture in England and Wales incorporates several elements that seem to be predicated on the assumption that ability is fixed. Commercial tests of cognitive abilities are used by many schools in Year 7 to predict the grades that students will get at GCSE. Test items are chosen pragmatically to correlate with examination performance in large samples rather than to support the analysis of misconceptions and identification of individual learning needs. When such tests are used to set targets for teachers, low expectations may be reinforced. Releasing such predictions to students would re-confirm a belief in their lack of innate ability in many cases, with dire consequences for self-efficacy and motivation.

Similarly, internal school examinations are likely to demotivate low-attaining students and to reconfirm the absolute nature of their low ability if they emphasize competition and performance. A focus on formative functions and personal development is necessary to ameliorate such negative impacts. If students are to feel motivated to work in preparation for examinations, they must attribute their success or failure to controllable factors such as effort or revision, rather than uncontrollable factors such as bad luck or lack of ability (Bandura 1977; Black 1998a; Wolters and Rosenthal 2000).

As we discussed in Chapter 4, metacognitive knowledge helps students to be aware of their strengths, weaknesses and what they do not fully understand, and thereby to identify aspects for focused learning. To maximize the effectiveness of their revision, however, their metacognitive knowledge also has to include the form that the assessment will take, the nature of a good answer, and the way marks will be allocated. Metacognitive knowledge does not develop unconsciously. It requires reflection, self-assessment and analysis. This requires conscious effort and the application of effective learning strategies.

Children need to be aware of effective strategies for reviewing and revising their work and analysing their successes and failures. For example, they need to have strategies for planning and engaging in revision, identifying key features of their work and anticipating potential difficulties in advance of assessment. After assessment they require strategies for analysing and evaluating their performance. And finally, they must be inclined to implement these strategies in the belief that their performance will improve (Gipps 1994; Tanner and Jones 1994; Brookhart 2001; Tanner and Jones 2003b, c).

Although some high-attaining students possess some of these attributes, many of your students will not. A recent questionnaire study of over 300 students from six schools about their learning of mathematics in Key Stage 3 revealed that there is significant room for improvement in the ways that children prepare for examinations and use the feedback afterwards (Tanner and Jones 2003b). The survey revealed that a substantial minority of students held beliefs, that would be likely to have a negative impact on their future learning. For example, 28 per cent of the sample agreed with the statement 'Some people just can't do maths'. Similarly, 21 per cent agreed with 'You can either do maths or you can't'.

Success in examinations was generally attributed to hard work (84 per cent) or doing lots of revision (71 per cent), but a substantial minority of students blamed their failure on uncontrollable factors such as poor memory (24 per cent), being unlucky with the questions (20 per cent) or having no natural ability in mathematics (14 per cent). However, even though the majority of students expressed positive beliefs and attitudes towards revision, other factors suggest that they are unlikely to apply their efforts to best effect (Tanner and Jones 2003b).

Although 75 per cent of students claimed to know which parts of mathematics they did not understand, only 57 per cent claimed to know which mistakes they were most likely to make. Worryingly, 47 per cent reported that they often get a question wrong but don't understand why, and only 40 per cent have the confidence to claim that they know when they have got a question right. This suggests a lack of depth in metacognitive knowledge that is likely to limit the efficiency of revision. It also suggests that the formative feedback loop has not operated effectively for a significant number of students. Students need a detailed knowledge of their strengths and weaknesses to regulate their learning effectively.

Although two-thirds of students claimed to revise before tests and examinations, worryingly only 59 per cent tried to understand where they went wrong if they made a mistake in their work. A substantial minority of students did not attempt to make any formative use of the feedback they received. When students attribute their success or failure to uncontrollable factors, they are unlikely to try to learn from their mistakes.

The efficiency of the students' revision strategies was dubious. Only 51 per cent claimed to be aware of a variety of revision strategies. The most commonly used revision strategies were passive or reactive in character, rather than pro-active. 'Reading through their books' was the most popular strategy (73 per cent), and the only strategy used by many students. A similar problem was reported by KMOFAP, with students using passive revision techniques and not transferring the active learning strategies they were using in school to the work they were doing at home (Black, et al. 2003, p. 53). Passive revision strategies do not require active processing and are unlikely to impact significantly on learning.

More effective revision strategies were used by only a minority of students: making revision notes (44 per cent), doing lots of questions (41 per cent), writing some questions to test myself (39 per cent), highlighting the most important parts of my work (34 per cent), or trying to predict what the questions will ask (20 per cent). All these strategies require some degree of metacognitive knowledge and, given the lack of depth in their metacognitive knowledge reported above, it is perhaps not surprising that they were used more infrequently.

The students' strategies for learning from examinations were also quite limited in many cases. Most students claimed to make sure that they understood their mistakes (69 per cent); worked out how to do better next time (65 per cent); and worked out where they were going wrong (61 per cent). However, given that many (55 per cent) admitted that they only looked at their marks when getting their examination papers back, the validity of their claims for reviewing their learning must be dubious. This is in accord with the results of Butler's research (1987, 1988), with the formative functions of the assessment being drowned out by a focus on performance, marks and grades. In such circumstances the desire of many students to 'work out how to do better next time' is likely to be restricted to unfocused targets like 'try harder' or 'be more careful'.

If tests and examinations are to be used formatively, students need to analyse their work closely, identify specific areas where learning or understanding is incomplete and set themselves precise personal targets. These must be specific learning targets such as 'Learn the names of the original 13 American colonies', rather then performance targets such as 'Try to get a grade C next time'. Although some high-attaining students are aware of such strategies and use them regularly, many other students need to be taught how to use them. For many low-attaining students, receiving back examination papers is emotionally challenging and serves only to confirm their belief that they are just not clever enough.

There are strong correlations between self-efficacy, metacognition and the use of self-regulated learning strategies (Tanner and Jones 2003b). Causality is probably complex, although, we would suggest that students who believe that their ability is not fixed and that their performance in examinations is due to controllable factors are more likely to employ effective learning and revision strategies than those who attribute success or failure to luck or lack of ability.

As we discussed in Chapter 4, metacognitive knowledge is not fixed and may be developed through the use of learning strategies such as 'working out what I don't know' and 'highlighting the important parts of my work'. These are also effective revision strategies, and students with good metacognitive knowledge are likely to revise more effectively.

More effective revision is likely to lead to improved performance in examinations and develop or reinforce a belief that ability is not fixed but developmental. The successful application of effective learning strategies is likely to encourage the development of self-efficacy. The resulting virtuous circle (see Figure 5.1) may become self-perpetuating (Tanner and Jones 2003b).

Unfortunately, for many students a vicious circle may develop (Figure 5.2). Students who lack self-efficacy and who believe that they lack natural ability are unlikely to apply effective learning and revision strategies or develop metacognitive knowledge. Their failure to revise effectively may then lead to repeated failure in examinations. This reduces self-efficacy and may then reinforce 'a shared belief between them and their teacher that they are just not clever enough' (Black 1998b).

Breaking into this vicious circle is difficult, but we would suggest that attempts be made to teach all students the self-regulated learning strategies that are known by the successful minority of reflective and metacognitively skilled students (Tanner and Jones 2003b). Students need to be taught how to analyse their work to identify what is important, where they

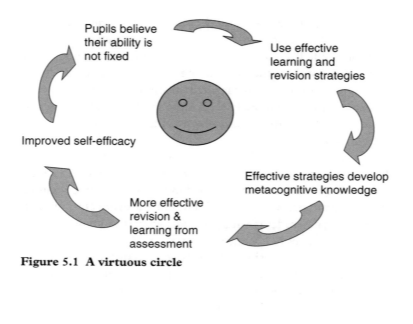

Pupils believe their ability is not fixed

Use effective learning and revision strategies

Improved self-efficacy

Effective strategies develop metacognitive knowledge

More effective revision & learning from assessment

**Figure 5.1  A virtuous circle**

Low self-efficacy & belief in lack of natural ability

Failure to apply effective learning strategies

Reinforcement of belief that they are just not clever enough

Regular failure in assessments

**Figure 5.2  A vicious circle**

are likely to make mistakes, how to make effective notes and how they can improve their work. They also need to be taught how to prepare for examinations, learning the nature of good answers and how to gain maximum marks for their work. They need to learn how to analyse the resulting feedback from examinations to identify strategies and targets for improvement. Teaching these strategies directly should help to develop a formative assessment culture that can use examinations to support learning.

## Teaching students to learn from summative assessment

The Developing Effective Revision Strategies (DERS) project was funded by the General Teaching Council for Wales (GTCW) in 2002–03. DERS used an action research design and was based on two professional networks of teacher researchers, one working in Key Stage 3 (six schools) and the other in Key Stage 4 (four schools). The professional networks were teacher-led and supported by ourselves, the authors, as university researchers who visited schools, observed lessons and facilitated network meetings.

As the project's name suggests, its main aim was to investigate how students could be helped to develop effective revision strategies. However, it should be emphasized that this was not about teaching children how to cram for examinations – far from it: our focus was on the learning process. Our intention was to develop and explore teaching approaches that would encourage students to analyse their own strengths and weaknesses and then employ effective strategies to progress their learning. Central to this process was the need to establish a formative assessment culture in which students developed positive beliefs about their ability to improve their own learning performance.

The students involved were mainly in Year 9 and Year 11, so high-stakes external examinations were clearly a high priority for both students and teachers. As a consequence, some of the strategies we used focused on the style of question expected in the forthcoming Key Stage 3 and GCSE examinations. However, the aim was to develop attitudes, knowledge, skills and strategies, which would support lifelong learning rather than just improve performance in an examination.

One of the leading teacher researchers had been developing formative assessment strategies in his school for several years. His approaches formed a focus for our initial discussions and interventions. Our discussions were also informed by the strategies used in KMOFAP (Black, et al. 2003) and earlier projects of our own (e.g.: Tanner and Jones 1994, 1999). The action research methodology was exploratory and based on local design, in that the teacher researchers devised and refined individual action plans as they explored ways of integrating selected strategies into their own practices. As the project progressed, strategies were developed further in the context of the teacher researchers' own schools, and new strategies were devised and investigated (Tanner and Jones 2003b).

The strategies may be grouped under three main themes. The first theme was metacognitive in character and demanded that students articulate their thinking about their work and make realistic assessments of their strengths and weaknesses, identifying areas of potential difficulty. The second theme was more closely focused on the demands of the examination and encouraged students to internalize assessment criteria so that they came to understand the nature of a good solution and were able to assess their current performance against the ideal. The third theme focused on the strategies, which could be employed after tests and examinations to identify misconceptions, analyse errors and devise action plans. Underpinning all of these themes, however, was the regularly articulated belief that all students could succeed through their own efforts and that ability was not fixed but was trainable.

## The strategies for developing self-efficacy

Our aim was that the students would learn to behave differently, and more importantly think differently, both about their capacity for, and their relationship with learning. We wanted them to begin taking active responsibility for their own learning and applying significant effort to review and reflect, not only prior to end-of-unit tests and school examinations, but also as a feature of their normal learning behaviours.

Change of this order is unlikely to be sustained unless students believe in the initiative and quickly see hard evidence of success in their own terms (Fullan 1991). To this end teachers began the project with a serious effort to convince their students of the value of review and reflection on their work and revision for tests and examinations. We had to convince students that they were all capable of learning more effectively and that their future attainment depended on their application of effective learning strategies rather than their ability.

Most of the teachers began their intervention with what they referred to as the 'David Beckham' lesson, in which they discussed his corner kicking prowess and tried to convince students that ability and success are not innate, but built on hard work and training. Skill in taking corners is based on practising taking corners, not a corner kicking gene!

Some teachers, recognizing the need for students to see the value of revision from an early stage, deliberately made the first assessment after the project had started somewhat easier than usual so that everyone could see improved performance and attribute it to new ways of revising!

However, one lesson or one assessment is not enough. Developing self-efficacy is a long, slow process and is more a matter of developing classroom ethos and the socialization of students into an effective learning culture than use of a particular strategy. The message must be implicit in every teaching strategy and explicit in many.

## Metacognitive strategies: Review, reflection and revision notebooks

The first strategy, which all the teachers implemented, was the creation of a separate revision notebook by students. In order to generate enthusiasm for the project and to emphasize personal ownership, the notebooks were chosen to appear different from standard exercise books, and unusual rules applied to them. For example, the use of coloured highlighter pens and bubble writing was allowed, and students were encouraged to express their ownership of the books by decorating and organizing them as they saw fit.

Students were given a revision list based on the examination or unit syllabus. They were then asked to make up between five and ten pages of revision notes and examples, according to the age and experience of the class. The students were expected to find appropriate examples for themselves that would cover the range of the work. Examples could be chosen from a variety of sources such as textbooks, classwork, the Internet, etc., as well as being invented by the students themselves. A balance was demanded between worked examples and notes.

All work was expected to be annotated and not just copied out. Pupils' annotations had to explain the methods they were using and note 'warnings' to themselves indicating where they might make mistakes. The annotations had to be coloured differently to notes and examples. Typical annotations included:

- 'Be careful to cancel down here';
- 'Put all the Xs on the side which makes the total positive';
- 'Try to find a number they both divide into'.

A policy of zero tolerance operated if work was not completed to length and on time. Students soon learned how to spread work out, drawing large diagrams and showing all their working (usually a difficult thing to achieve!). Although some students objected to producing such notes and examples when they should have been 'getting on with their revision' (sic), eventually they began to appreciate that they were learning more effectively and most even began to appreciate being forced to revise. In some school sub-cultures it is easier to work hard when you can claim to have no choice.

> 'I'd recommend this revision to all students in any school. It has helped me a lot and boosted my grades. If I [hadn't been] told to do it and it wasn't made compulsory, I wouldn't have done it.'
> Year II boy

One problem that arose with some classes was a reluctance of some students to write revision notes for an examination that seemed to be some distance away. (Not all schools used end-of-unit assessment.) For these classes, the book was re-titled as a reflection book, which had to be updated on a regular basis. When school tests and examinations occurred on a long cycle, e.g.: half yearly or yearly, the task of creating a revision book immediately prior to examination would be too daunting to be effective. We aimed instead to build up revision/reflection notebooks gradually, perhaps focusing on a topic at a time. The amount of work that students should summarize into notes, examples and annotations depends on the nature of the topic, the frequency of lessons and the background of the class. A pragmatic decision was taken by teachers about the size of the task that was most appropriate for their class, and varied between a week and a month's work.

Part of the value of writing revision books rests in students reviewing earlier work and identifying the most important ideas, concepts and processes. The very act of selecting suitable examples to represent the knowledge being learned forced students to consider the range of the topic and to focus on the key issues. They did not find this easy at first, being used to being spoon-fed tasks without having to consider their purpose or place in the overall picture of the subject. Consequently, in the early stages, students' notes were often regurgitated examples from classwork or copied from textbooks, with very few examples of their own. Summarizing a topic into a concise set of notes and examples is not a straightforward skill: rather it is a learned behaviour and, we would suggest, one that should be taught actively. Of course there is little time in the crowded curriculum to add a new topic. However, we would not advocate note-taking as a de-contextualized topic, but rather as something which should develop from the collective reflection that should occur in plenary sessions at the end of lessons and modules of work.

Several teachers modified their plenary sessions to help students to develop such skills. The annotation of revision notes and examples was supported by asking students to summarize the key points from the lesson, and the identification of tips and hints warning other students of potential difficulties soon became a regular feature of many plenaries. Some teachers formalized such skills further by asking students to work in groups to create 'end-of-module tips' posters for classroom display. Some teachers also encouraged students to produce 'mind maps' of topics. At the end of a unit of work they would be asked to think about all the concepts and ideas linked to the topic. These might be links within the topic, links to other aspects of the subject or possible applications in real life. Some teachers used a double page in the notebook, while others created A3 posters for classroom display and used them as stimuli for discussion. The aim was to construct knowledge that was connected rather than isolated and, therefore, more likely to be memorable and useable (Roberts 2004).

Students quickly realized the value of annotating work and began to include annotations, warnings and explanations in their normal exercise books without being asked.

'It's good to do notes as well because when you look back and think, "How did I do that?" the notes remind you.'

Year II pupil

The reflection/revision books quickly became a significant part of the written output for the intervention classes, and began to replace more routine forms of homework. The issue then arose as to how the work should be marked or feedback given. In this matter the teacher researchers often felt constrained by school policy or by concerns that pages of student-generated writing would appear to be unmarked. To mark all of the notes produced in detail would be impractical – the volume was too great, and the task became particularly onerous when students made up their own examples.

Some teachers felt obliged to grade revision books against criteria relating to the accuracy, detail, explanation, presentation and variety of examples. Most felt that the principle of personal ownership and the research of Butler (1987, 1988) led them to avoid grades and only offer feedback in the form of formative suggestions for improvement.

However, the possibility of inaccurate notes being uncorrected remained, as students generated ever larger volumes of notes. One strategy used by some teachers was to demand that the first example on each topic be taken from a reliable source such as a textbook and that this example be given considerable annotation. This could then be checked in detail for any misconceptions. If problems were apparent, the remaining work was then checked in detail.

Some teachers checked the accuracy of pupil examples by using them in an end-of-lesson game in which one side of the class challenged the other to answer the questions they had set. Responsibility had to rest with the student, however, to monitor their own understanding, to check out any uncertainties and to ensure that their revision books were accurate.

Some teachers used students' reflective comments to generate class discussions at the start of the next lesson, particularly when a misconception had been identified. Sometimes, students were invited to share their reflections and examples in class for peer discussion and evaluation (Roberts 2004).

## Preparation for examinations

The strategies described above are focused on learning rather than examination performance. However, our work took place in the context of high-stakes external examination in Year 9 and Year 11, and the revision/review books gained some of their status with students as a resource that would eventually help to improve their examination performance. With that in mind, some of the strategies used were targeted on learning to perform well in examinations.

One of the key features of the review books was the inclusion of examples that had been invented by the student. Requiring students to devise their own questions has two distinct aims. As we indicated in Chapter 4, our main aim was to give students greater insight into the structure of problems within their subject. A secondary aim here was for students to recognize the way such questions are usually presented in an external examination and develop an understanding of the way mark schemes operate.

Small groups of students were asked to look at past papers and to devise questions in the style of the examination. They were also asked to devise an appropriate mark scheme. When the target examination was an internal one, some teachers added an element of competition to the process by offering to include the best question in the actual paper! Others collected in student-devised questions and selected a few of the best to use as a class task at the start of the next lesson. After attempting each other's questions, they were self-marked according to the students' mark schemes. Class discussion then followed about the nature of a good question, the nature of a good solution and the way marks were distributed in the mark scheme. In doing this, students learned what examiners were looking for and how to optimize their performance. It also helped them to identify areas they could target for improvement. Furthermore, they rehearsed a revision strategy that was more effective than just reading through their books! Students who prepare for examinations by devising and answering their own questions out-perform control groups who revise in other more traditional ways (King 1992; Foos, *et al.* 1994; Black, *et al.* 2003).

Some students even wrote whole examination papers for themselves. One girl produced a trial examination paper on her computer at home including a cover page with the full official rubric in Welsh and English alongside the examination board logo! Her school internal examination result was excellent. Other students attributed her success to her revision effort and more students became motivated to try the same.

The 'traffic-light' strategy (see Chapter 4) was adapted to support revision. To help students to plan and target their revision more effectively, KMOFAP asked students to annotate a list of keywords taken from the examination syllabus with traffic lights – green for areas in which their knowledge is secure, amber for an area they are unsure about and red for areas they don't understand. This formed the basis for a personal revision plan targeted at areas of weakness rather than secure knowledge. KMOFAP also reported using peer tutoring, in which groups of students selected questions from past papers that targeted their red or amber areas and then worked together to find solutions (Black, *et al.* 2003).

Similar strategies were used in the DERS project. Revision books were annotated with traffic lights in the same way. Some teachers paired off greens and ambers on specific topics to support each other, while targeting reds themselves. The annotated examples in the revision books provided a resource for peer working.

# Post-examination review

After examinations and module tests had occurred, major effort was invested in returning scripts to students for analysis, reflection and target setting. The 'traffic-lights' approach was used successfully by several teachers, with students annotating their returned scripts to identify specific areas for remediation. Sometimes, peer tutoring was used with amber-green pairs and teacher guidance for reds.

Some teachers also analysed examination scripts, identifying the common errors and misconceptions that were made and planning to modify future teaching accordingly. This strategy also allowed teachers to focus on key learning targets when reviewing papers with their classes. Such analysis is time consuming, but time can be gained by extending the peer- and self-marking strategies, described in Chapter 4, to examination scripts.

KMOFAP asked small groups of students to agree on a good answer to one of the examination questions before devising a mark scheme (Black, et al. 2003). Following discussion, scripts were returned for students to peer- or self-mark. Some teachers on the DERS project ensured that only test scripts and a red pen were on desks, to maintain a degree of security. The most problematic questions were then discussed in detail with a view to improving performance. Peer- and self-marking helped students to understand the nature of a good solution and the kind of response to which examiners would give credit. Understanding how mark schemes worked helped students to understand how their answers might have been structured more effectively.

The most important message to be conveyed in the aftermath of an examination was that the mark gained should not be regarded as the end of the process, but rather the starting point for the next phase of learning.

## The impact of the DERS project

Qualitative data on the success of the strategies was collected through interviews with students and teachers, and observation of lessons. The project was short-lived (four months in total), but even within that short timescale positive changes in attitude and behaviour began to appear in most classes.

> 'Some people find maths harder than others but that doesn't mean they can't do it. They have to put more effort into it so they can learn more things.'
>
> Year 9 student

Comments from students revealed that they were convinced about the value of their revision notebooks and intended to continue using them:

> 'To help a friend with low marks to revise I'd tell them to make notes like these. When you look back at your revision book you know the key points because you've underlined them, and I'd say to write them out, and look at the example to see what the teacher means, and then you can get a better understanding.'
>
> Year 10 student

The local design and exploratory action research nature of the project limited the potential for systematic quantitative evaluation of the strategies. However, one of the teacher researchers involved conducted a study comparing two parallel Year 8 Set 2 mathematics classes that she taught over a module of work lasting nine lessons (Roberts 2004). Both classes were taught the same work, but one class used the following formative assessment strategies:

1. Students writing review notes about what they learned in the lesson.

2. Students writing 'help' notes to assist other students' understanding.

3. Students generating their own revision questions.

4. Students creating their own mind maps to aid revision.

The classes were given a pre-test, before teaching, a post-test immediately after teaching and a delayed test eight weeks later. They were also given an attitude questionnaire assessing their self-efficacy each time.

Even after only nine lessons, the intervention class scored significantly higher than the control class on self-efficacy ($p < 0.03$). The intervention class outperformed the control class in both the post-test ($p < 0.03$) and the delayed test ($p < 0.01$). Although the sample was small ($n = 60$) and the intervention relatively short (nine lessons) Roberts' (2004) results confirm the qualitative data from the DERS project: that middle band students can learn how to learn effectively from summative assessment. Similarly, KMOFAP demonstrate that an emphasis on formative assessment strategies focused on learning rather than performance in high-stakes summative examinations can lead to real and significant improvements in students' learning (Black, et al. 2003).

In the end, assessment is only valuable if it changes the way teachers teach and students learn. The most important end user of assessment information is not the government but the student. If our students are to develop into effective lifelong learners, they must come to believe in their ability to change and learn the habits of formative self-assessment. As we have indicated in the preceding chapters, this is dependent on the development of a formative assessment culture in your school or department: and it is to this that we now turn.

# 6

# Developing an effective learning culture: Strategies for change

We hope you are now beginning to be enthusiastic about developing your own pedagogy and introducing aspects of Assessment for Learning (AfL) into your own practice. In this chapter we aim to offer practical advice about changing yourself and your institution.

Unlike many initiatives in education, the introduction of AfL would seem to hold the promise of considerable learning gains (Black and Wiliam 1998a, b). Furthermore, AfL is unusual in that what is sometimes referred to as 'scientific evidence' from academic researchers in inauthentic settings, and the evidence from practitioners and teacher-researchers in real school settings, are generally aligned and mutually supportive (Hargreaves 2004). Because of the supporting evidence, in many schools and local authorities AfL is this year's good idea. The QCA website offers considerable advice in support of AfL and a version (some would say perversion) of it is central to the Key Stage 3 Strategy in England (Hargreaves 2004, p. 9).

However, tensions exist between the current permeating culture of high-stakes summative assessment and the formative functions of assessment. Although we demonstrated in the last chapter that examinations could be used formatively, this is only viable within a learning culture that prioritizes the learning process over examination performance and the needs of the learner over the needs of the curriculum. Although AfL is included in the KS3 strategy, much of the associated guidance emphasizes curriculum delivery rather than learning and understanding.

Formative assessment has been used to describe a wide variety of practices over the years, and the term is still ill-defined in

101

practice. Torrance and Pryor (1998, p. 153) make a useful distinction between convergent and divergent versions of formative assessment (see Table 6.1).

Convergent formative assessment is focused on the needs of the curriculum and whether the student has met its demands. It aims to identify the parts of the curriculum that the student cannot perform, identifying the gap so it can be filled. It is done by the teacher to the pupil and is based on a behaviourist view of learning. It is little more than repeated summative assessment to

**Table 6.1 Characteristics of convergent and divergent formative assessment**

| Convergent formative assessment | Divergent formative assessment |
|---|---|
| Aims to discover *whether* the learner knows, understands or can do a pre-determined thing | Aims to discover *what* the learner knows, understands and can do |
| Precise planning | Flexible planning |
| Tick lists and can-do statements | Open forms of recording |
| Analysed from point of view of curriculum | Analysed from point of view of learner and the curriculum |
| Closed or pseudo-open questioning and tasks | Open questioning and tasks |
| Focus on contrasting errors with correct responses | Focus on miscues and prompting metacognition |
| Judgemental or quantitative evaluation | Descriptive rather than purely judgemental evaluation |
| Pupil as recipient of assessment | Pupil as initiator as well as recipient |
| Behaviourist view of learning | Constructivist view of learning |
| Intention to teach next thing in linear progression | Intention is to teach in zone of proximal development |
| Assessment accomplished by the teacher | Assessment accomplished jointly by the teacher and the pupil |
| Repeated summative assessment or continuous assessment | Accepts the complexity of formative assessment |

(Summarized from Torrance and Pryor 1998, p. 153)

monitor and control the student's trajectory through the curriculum. The main user of the feedback is the teacher who uses it to plan future teaching. Its introduction would represent little more than a marginal or superficial change in current practice for many schools and teachers.

Divergent formative assessment is focused on the needs of the learner within the context of the curriculum. It aims to analyse the students' current understanding and develop their metacognitive knowledge. It is accomplished collaboratively between students and teachers and is based on a constructivist view of learning. It recognizes the complex nature of true formative assessment and is intended to assist students in taking responsibility for their own learning. The teacher uses feedback to plan future teaching, but its main purpose is to develop students' metacognitive knowledge and help them to plan future learning. For most schools and teachers this would represent a radical change in current practices.

It is divergent formative assessment that we have been developing the case for in this book, and which is most likely to lead to learning gains. Unfortunately, the prevailing high-stakes summative assessment culture tends to encourage the convergent form at the expense of student learning.

Student learning is at the heart of AfL. This sounds uncontentious until you reflect on the extent to which assessment policies have been geared towards 'the delivery' of the National Curriculum, the selection and certification of students, accountability and the management of the system since the 1980s. On reflection, it is frightening how little attention has been paid to the learning needs of students during that period. The change being proposed here is radical, not marginal.

First, you should recognize that the version of AfL that we have described in the preceding chapters represents a deep change in practice for most teachers. Introducing AfL is not a 'quick fix' and involves much more than the addition of few 'bolt-on' strategies to your current assessment practices. The potential rewards will only come about if you are able to accommodate the underlying ideas into your pedagogical practices in a meaningful and coherent manner. This can only happen relatively slowly with conscious intent and monitoring on your part.

Underpinning the inroduction of AfL is the development of an effective formative assessment culture, and a change in the way that teachers and learners view their relative roles and responsibilities. It is a slow and cumulative change as formative assessment gradually moves to the centre of the learning process. It was described by some KMOFAP teachers as 'scary', with control and responsibility for learning moved away from the teacher and towards the students as collaborative responsibility grew (Black, *et al.* 2003).

Ideally, the development of a formative assessment culture should be a whole-school initiative. It is difficult, although not impossible, to develop a learning culture in one class that runs counter to the prevailing culture of the school. The research we reported in Chapter 3 by Smith and Gorad (2005) on the introduction of comments-only marking in just one form group demonstrates the difficulties. The class that experienced comments-only marking were part of a year group that received marks as a norm and considered they were missing out. However, it is possible to begin to explore some of the strategies in a single class if conditions are sufficiently favourable, as the research study by Roberts (2004) shows. In the following sections we will examine strategies for introducing formative assessment at the level of your classroom, your department and your school.

## Introducing formative assessment in your classroom

Ideally, in order to explore the possibilities offered by formative assessment in your classroom, you should be taking part in a whole-school or departmental initiative. If this is not the case then you need to think carefully about which initiatives are practical to introduce in your context. Your first step should be to explore with your head of department which of the strategies we have discussed might be explored with an experimental class. If permission for this is not granted then you will be restricted to exploring aspects of formative assessment that are completely internal to your classroom, such as rich questioning or collective reflection in the plenary, while you apply for a new job!

If you are granted at least minimal indulgence to explore some strategies, you may be able to develop yourself as a 'Trojan horse' within your department, eventually demonstrating the power of formative assessment to the others through your success.

Our next suggestion is that you find a friend to talk to and work with. You will get feedback on your progress continually from your students, but you also need feedback from a fellow professional to help you to develop your professional skills. Ideally this should be a departmental colleague who is willing to explore alongside you, sharing the planning and developing ideas in a similar context.

One of the most effective forms of professional development is to participate in an action research network with other teachers who are working together to improve their practice. At its simplest level this could be just two teachers working together and acting as critical but supportive friends. However, there might be other teachers in your area who are willing to join you in a professional network funded by the General Teaching Council (GTC). You should also consider contacting your local higher education institutions and enquiring whether any of their staff would be interested in researching the introduction of formative assessment strategies with you. Often it is possible to arrange to observe other teachers trying to introduce such strategies in return for being observed yourself. The professional feedback you receive from such visits is invaluable. The benefits of formative assessment apply to your learning too! You should regard yourself as an independent learner/researcher in need of formative feedback to inform your future planning.

If your school culture has over-emphasized high-stakes competitive summative assessment in response to government initiatives over the years, you may think that your established practices are inevitable. Your first task should be to stand back and reflect on the purpose and efficacy of your current assessment practices, evaluating the extent to which they support the learning process as opposed to managerial or communicative aims. Is the balance right?

We suggest that you use following prompts to stimulate reflection on your own teaching practices. You might like to use the traffic-light strategy on the list, using green for 'I am happy with my practice in this area', amber for 'I have made some progress but could develop further' and red for 'I am not happy with my practice in this area'.

Consider the occasions when you assess formally through tests:

- Do students revise effectively for your tests?

- Have you discussed with them how to revise?

- Are they able to identify for themselves where they as individuals need to focus their learning and revision before the test?

- Do your test questions assess higher order thinking or routine skills?

- Are your questions targeted at specific misconceptions or do they mimic standard exercise questions?

- After the test, do you discuss with students what a good solution would look like?

- After the test, do they analyse their errors and try to correct them or do they just look at their position in the rank order?

- Do you analyse their errors as a part of your lesson planning?

- Are your tests timetabled so that errors and misconceptions that are exposed can be addressed before the end of the module?

- After the test, do you help your students to set learning targets for themselves by providing specific guidance in comments, or do you just give marks?

- Do you know why you are testing? Is it mainly to support learning or to provide a summative mark for a record?

When you mark students' work:

- Do you regularly mark some of their work in depth with detailed comments?

- Do your comments advise about the nature of a good answer?

- Do your comments offer specific guidance on how to move learning forwards?

- Do you give students time to read, reflect and act on your comments when work is returned?

- Do some of your comments lead to a dialogue between you and the student?

- Do students set themselves personal short-term learning targets when marked work is returned?

When you are teaching, how often do you:

- Plan your lesson in terms of learning goals rather than tasks to complete?

- Share your learning goals with the class?

- Allow children sufficient time to think before demanding a response?

- Ask a question that requires an extended answer of two or three sentences?

- Ask children to explain their thinking rather than just demanding a factual or procedural response?

- Ask a question that has a range of possible answers to encourage discussion?

- Encourage children to debate alternative positions on an issue?

- Really listen to students' ideas and respect their opinions?

- Use a student's idea to take the lesson in a slightly different direction for a while?

- Allow time for children to reflect for themselves about what has been learned rather than summarizing the key points yourself?

- Discuss assessment criteria with your class?

- Encourage children to assess themselves?

- Encourage independent learning?

How often do children in your classes:

- Speak in sentences rather than offering single-word answers?

- Make an utterance of more than ten seconds duration to the whole class?

- Come to see you about a question they don't understand outside the lesson?

- Volunteer to you exactly what it is they know they don't understand?

- Assess themselves?

- Write their own revision notes rather than just copying down your notes?

- Seem to be dependent on you to lead them all the time?

- Seem to think that they're just not clever enough to succeed?

Although you may have identified several areas for development from the lists above, you cannot make progress on them all at once. We suggest that you begin by identifying one important area in which change would not be in obvious conflict with current school policy.

If your ultimate aim is to develop a formative assessment culture in your classroom, this is likely to involve radical changes in your role, the role of your students, and your expectations of your students. This carries risks as well as rewards, and change can be unsettling. We would suggest that you choose a class with which you already have a good relationship and that are not too set in their ways. Students who are close to a high-stakes examination are unlikely to appreciate a radical change in classroom culture! Year 7 is often a good choice as they arrive in secondary school not knowing exactly what to expect and are likely to accept the new regime as being the norm in their new environment.

We suggest that you start by introducing strategies that will improve the quality of learning and teaching without making dramatic changes to the locus of control in your classroom. For example, introducing rich questioning based on misconceptions and extended answers will allow you to begin to increase children's responsibilities within the lesson and to be seen to be taking their opinions seriously. This can be combined easily with an increase in 'wait time' and perhaps experimenting with 'no hands-up'.

One important aspect for evaluation is the extent to which your lessons are planned around learning rather than tasks and activities. Although when you were a student teacher you were probably asked to write lesson plans that began with aims and objectives, research suggests that many experienced teachers plan their lessons around the tasks that are to be completed during the lesson (Tanner and Jones 2000b; Wragg 2005). In many cases this is because experienced teachers have long since internalized the aims of the activities they use and are focusing pragmatically on organizational matters. However, the original aims of activities may not have been considered for many years and, because of this, practice may have drifted off target over time. Re-visiting and re-evaluating the learning aims of the activities you use is a helpful strategy for developing your practice.

For example, although discussion and experimentation may be the most appropriate way to develop an understanding of particular scientific concepts, copying out definitions and diagrams produces more apparent work in students' books and is easier to control. Similarly, although the original aim might have been for students to learn how to investigate, make decisions and plan for themselves, telling them exactly how to organize their work makes the completion of the task easier. In both these examples, for pragmatic reasons, the original learning aims have been subverted to the false aim of completing tasks. Although a quiet classroom may result and students' books may fill up with neat writing and diagrams, what has been generated is often apparent rather than genuine learning.

When a summative assessment culture dominates, students often seem to conspire to maintain poor practices that focus on task completion, mark generation and the collection of merit awards, rather than learning – it is far easier to mindlessly complete routine tasks than to explore, think, problem-solve and plan your own learning. Introducing a divergent formative assessment culture demands radical changes of your students' learning behaviours as well as your teaching styles. That is the whole point! However, this means that students must understand what you are trying to achieve and agree to join you on the journey. Sharing the aims of your lessons with your class is often seen as a first step in this process (AAIA 2002).

Stating learning objectives at the start of a lesson is coming to be regarded as good practice, with some classes even having a separate 'objectives' board for this purpose. This can be re-visited in the plenary to compare actual learning with the intended learning and check whether 'the gap has been closed'. This convergent version of formative assessment often seems to miss the point. When oversimplified learning objectives are viewed in a behaviourist manner, pace and curriculum coverage may be emphasized at the expense of understanding. A resulting lack of flexibility often excludes genuine collaborative learning. For example, a learning objective like 'discover that steel is attracted by a magnet' precludes the possibility of true experimentation or exploration.

It may sound heretical in the current climate, but we sometimes like to keep our learning objectives secret at the start of the lesson so that we can explore together and arrive at an unexpected and exciting conclusion with a degree of showmanship! The issue is more to do with developing a collaborative learning culture than obeying a standard format of learning objectives and plenary activities. In a collaborative learning culture, although you, as the teacher, must be sure about the general trajectory of learning, there must be sufficient flexibility in planning to allow students to become genuinely engaged in the co-construction of knowledge. This may often involve the generation of shared learning objectives. The intention should be to leave room for the learner's input.

A divergent formative assessment culture makes significant demands upon the effort and degree of engagement that your students make in lessons. Our experience is that they are willing to make the effort only if they see a positive return in their own terms. Eventually, your aim should be that the returns are intrinsic to the subject and result in interest and empowerment. In the end, you want your students to learn because they value and enjoy learning. However, realistically it takes a long time to develop such a culture, and in the short term, they must gain rewards that they value today. We suggest that you manipulate assessment, like the teachers in the DERS project, ensuring early success so that students feel empowered by the new strategies and begin to believe that they are able to learn and succeed in your subject.

One of the most powerful strategies that you may choose to introduce is the use of review/revision books. These books have the advantage that they focus on learning and begin to empower students from the start. They make your students feel special and are quickly appreciated. However, as we indicated in Chapter 5, students need to learn skills of reflection and self-monitoring to use them effectively. Their effective use is facilitated if students have experienced creating their own questions and writing help notes for imaginary students. And, as we indicated in Chapter 4, experience of peer-assessment should precede self-assessment.

Although formative assessment is not an add-on process, but demands deep pedagogical changes, introducing such strategies into your classroom can begin to create a climate of learning. Greater impact is achieved, however, if such approaches are adopted across the department.

## Developing a formative assessment culture in your department

If you are a head of department, you may provide powerful leadership to enact changes likely to make a radical improvement to the quality of learning and teaching in your subject. This applies even if you are operating within a whole-school culture that is posited on high-stakes summative assessment. To some extent, students are able to accept that different rules and norms operate within the different subjects they meet in secondary school.

If you intend to introduce formative assessment practices in your department as a part of a school policy initiative, we hope that you believe in the initiative and the proposed strategies. If you are unable to give the initiative your full personal support it is likely to flounder. The radical changes in pedagogy that are demanded will not be achieved if you are merely following orders. The same applies to the teachers in your department. It is your task to initiate a change that is supported in the hearts and minds of your team because, as with all worthwhile educational change, it cannot be forced.

To develop a formative assessment culture in your department is necessarily a complex and ill-defined task. Teaching based on formative assessment is not mechanical or formulaic, but requires creative decision-making on the part of skilled professionals. This cannot be mandated.

The form of curriculum management that is most appropriate for such a task has been characterized by Holt (1996) as the 'Casablanca model', after the famous film. The head of Warner Brothers studios, Jack Warner, knew that making good movies demanded initiative and creativity. He monitored the progress of each film by watching 'the rushes', but left the artistic control in the hands of his directors and actors. Similarly, although you are able to monitor the nature of some of the feedback being offered in your department, the organic nature of AfL means that you are unable control it directly.

The script of *Casablanca* was written from day-to-day as the filming progressed, and no one knew how the film would end until the airport sequence was filmed. It is worth noting that many of the best lines in *Casablanca* were unscripted, being ad-libbed by Bogart and Bergman as they interacted (e.g., 'Here's lookin' at you, kid'). We think the parallel with the management of AfL is very close indeed, in spite of the overly precise planning suggested by the framework.

The best teaching involves interaction. Teachers 'bounce off' pupils, making immediate decisions in response to the continuous feedback they are receiving (ad-libbing). Effective curriculum planning allows teachers to modify plans for tomorrow's lesson in the light of today's, within an overall framework of general aims and principles (day-to-day script writing). As head of department, you must ensure that your scheme of work indicates a trajectory of learning without becoming a straightjacket that constrains imaginative teaching from responding to students' needs. For example, we know of schools who have invested heavily in commercially-produced resources that provide precise lesson plans, PowerPoint slides, and worksheets that all teachers must follow on a lesson-by-lesson basis. It is difficult to imagine how AfL could be introduced under such an inflexible regime.

Similarly, your departmental assessment and marking policies may represent another straightjacket. Policies based on regular, competitive, summative assessments are likely to prevent the development of a formative assessment culture. We suggest that, before you ask members of your department to change their teaching practices, you review your current scheme of work and assessment policies to identify possible barriers to change. Policies in need of review could then be discussed at departmental meetings with regard to their impact on learning. New policies could then be developed collaboratively over the next year in parallel with experiences gained from exploring formative assessment strategies.

Implementing AfL represents a significant intrusion into pedagogical practices. It requires a fundamental change in underlying beliefs about what counts as good teaching (Black, *et al.* 2003). Teaching style is highly resistant to change, and is often claimed by teachers to be an expression of their personality (Goodson and Mangan 1995). Furthermore, the teachers in your department are probably operating very successfully according to their own standards and the usual norms of the school. Asking teachers to attempt to teach in different way is to ask them to take a risk with their professional reputations. Fortunately, the majority of teachers care deeply about their students and are interested in opening up new opportunities for them (Goodson and Mangan 1995).

Introducing AfL gives students a louder voice in the learning process, and for many teachers who struggle with classroom control, this can appear as a major issue. Furthermore, asking students to articulate their thinking and enter into discussion about fundamental principles can lead to some teachers finding the depth of their subject knowledge challenged. Students are also taking a risk by engaging with AfL and consenting to be questioned more rigorously, volunteering extended answers and potentially allowing their misconceptions to be exposed.

Such changes must be undertaken one step at a time, with full regard given to the risks. Teachers and students must quickly see some advantages resulting from their risk-taking – perhaps in improved examination performance, self-esteem or interest in lessons.

The complexity of the change is such that we would recommend that it is developed through action research. There is no 'bolt-on' approach that can be picked up and applied without modification. Teachers have to engage with the ideas and adapt them according to their own skills and beliefs. Ideally, action research groups should be composed of volunteers and you might set up a cadre group of volunteers from within your team. For example, you might all agree to experiment with one year group in the first instance. Even a pair of teachers working together could explore the issues profitably before reporting back to the department. Alternatively, you could work with teachers from another department. You could even involve another school if you gained funding from the GTC as suggested above.

The first action research cycle would involve each of the participating teachers modifying their current practice by adopting at least one of the classroom strategies listed above. They would reflect on their classroom experiences, evaluating their success, perhaps discussing the issues with trusted critical friends, perhaps in pairs. Ideally, such professional development should be supported by the provision of supply cover to facilitate observations of the practice of critical friends. Time should then be allocated at departmental meetings to discuss the impact of the initiatives. Effective heads of department ensure that pedagogical questions form the major agenda items at every departmental meeting. Routine communication of information should be relegated to memos rather than discussed in meetings (Tanner, *et al.* 2002). Following discussions, the strategies are modified or new strategies added, and the next action research cycle begins again.

To gain greatest impact from such research, however, it should be undertaken on a whole-school basis.

## Developing a formative assessment culture in your school

If you are a member of the senior management team in a secondary school, we would like to refer you back to our critique in Chapter 1 of the assessment practices at 'Standards Comprehensive' and the list of negative assessment practices commonly found in UK schools, so you can reconsider whether they apply to your own institution.

Government policies based upon the setting of benchmark targets such as the proportion of students gaining five A* to C at GCSE have had a distorting effect on views about the ultimate purpose of schools and education. We do not believe that examination success is the purpose of education – rather it is an indicator that education and learning *might* have occurred. Unfortunately, an overemphasis on examination performance can easily drive education and a love of learning out of the process.

Although large amounts of energy and resources in schools are spent on assessment, much of what is actually produced is at best educationally pointless, and at worst damaging to learning. Unless your school is unusual, a radical re-evaluation of your assessment practices may be needed.

Although the suggestions in the last two sections were aimed at teachers and heads of department, what is really called for are whole-school initiatives that build on these suggestions to change your school culture to one of collaborative learning and student responsibility rather than competitive performance and teacher dependency. What is required from senior managers is a commitment to transform learning through the development of divergent formative assessment strategies and a vision of schools as institutions that place learning, and learning to learn, at their heart.

We suggest that a strategy based on such a vision should begin with an audit of current policies and practices with a focus on the extent to which they support learning and the development of effective, lifelong learning skills. The audit might include the following issues:

- List all of the internal assessment demands that are placed on teachers and pupils each year and identify the purpose of each one as managerial, communicative, pedagogical or unclear.

- Which of the assessments that you described as managerial or communicative are really necessary? Could the data be gathered through assessments whose primary focus is formative? If not, how could their formative potential be enhanced?

- Do any of your assessment practices suggest to teachers or students that their ability is fixed and their potential performance predictable?

- How effective are the assessments that have pedagogical aims? How could they be made more effective? Could they form the basis of a strategy to develop a school culture based on AfL?

- Do any of your teachers or departments already utilize formative assessment strategies? Could they form the core of a cadre group to develop school policy?

- What assessment records are maintained? What are they used for? Are they worth the investment in terms of staff time and impact on student learning? Could they be scrapped or made more useful?

- Is student learning and the development of learning skills at the heart of school priorities? Or has this prime focus been lost in the pursuit of externally imposed targets?

We suggest that the audit should be a whole-school issue; that all staff should be aware that AfL will be at the heart of school development for the next few years and be involved in discussions about the vision of formative assessment that is intended. Based on the audit, a strategy should be developed to initiate changes in practice that will roll-out over an agreed, long-term timescale to change school culture in line with the shared vision and aims.

Some members of staff will be receptive to initiatives based on collaborative learning and increased student responsibility for their own learning. However, several others will feel personally threatened to various degrees because of arguments that we have rehearsed previously. Almost inevitably, some will continue to be resistant to change, while others will eventually be convinced by the success of other colleagues or the changed responses of students that they teach.

Given the complexity and personal involvement of all staff in the issues, we suggest that a development strategy be based initially on action research by a cadre group, perhaps in one year group or a small number of departments. Some of this group might be supported in studying for a higher degree whilst systematically evaluating the intervention.

We would also suggest that although the strategy must be home-grown and owned, stimulus inputs from LEA staff and local higher education institutions might be included where appropriate. An initiative on this scale should be evaluated formally and systematically. Academics from your local university Department of Education may be interested in helping to research the impact of the intervention and might be able to add useful contributions to discussions. The possibility of funding the development through GTC with academic support from a local University Department of Education should be considered.

In subsequent years, as the action research evolves, further strategies should be developed for evaluation and the cadre group expanded. A programme of planned expansion should eventually involve all teachers in the collaborative development of school policy on assessment and learning. This might be through the progressive inclusion of additional year groups or departments.

## Revisiting Standards Comprehensive

So how might Standards Comprehensive have changed a few years after introducing divergent formative assessment? We believe that it should have developed into a *learning school*. Learning to learn would be at the heart of the institution. The teaching would not be a one-size-fits-all model based on 'closing the gap' between students and an externally imposed standard. Rather, a 'bespoke tailoring' model of learning and teaching would apply, in which students and teachers collaborated to build on what was known.

Professionally confident teachers would feel empowered to base their decisions on student learning rather than curriculum coverage. Students would regard themselves as collaborators in the process and feel empowered to take responsibility for their own learning.

Improved examination results would be an outcome, but learning how to learn would be an ongoing process that convinced students that they were in control of their own destinies and able to learn through their own efforts. Similarly, teachers would be aware of strategies to investigate and develop their own professional practice and feel empowered to use them.

The nature and characteristics of formative assessment are still evolving. Schools and teacher researchers should be closely involved in creating the new consensus. In the end, the education community should value learning and aim to develop our children and ourselves as lifelong learners.

Assessment and learning? Mind the gap!

# References

Adey, P., and Shayer, M. (1993) 'An exploration of long-term far-transfer effects following an extended intervention in the high school science curriculum', *Cognition and Instruction*, 11(1), 1–29.

Association of Assessment Inspectors and Advisors (AAIA) (2002) *Secondary assessment practice: self evaluation and development materials*. http://www.aaia.org.uk/pdf/finalbooklet.PDF (accessed 6.9.05).

AifL (2005a) *Self/peer assessment: Greenock Academy, Inverclyde*. http://www.ltscotland.org.uk/assess/casestudies/index.asp?guidResource=4989 (accessed 6.9.05).

AifL (2005b) *Self/peer assessment: St Michael's academy, North Ayrshire*. http://www.ltscotland.org.uk/assess/casestudies/index.asp?guidResource=4993 (accessed 6.9.05).

Askew, M., Bliss, J., and Macrae, S. (1995) 'Scaffolding in mathematics, science, and technology', in P. Murphy, M. Selinger, J. Bourne, and M. Briggs (eds), *Subject Learning in the Primary Curriculum*. London: Routledge/OUP, pp. 209–17.

Askew, M., and Wiliam, D. (1995) *Recent Research in Mathematics Education 5–16*. London: HMSO.

Assessment Reform Group (ARG) (2002) *Assessment for learning: research-based principles to guide classroom practice*. http://arg.educ.cam.ac.uk/CIE3.pdf (accessed 31.8.05).

Bandura, A. (1977) 'Self efficacy: towards a unifying theory of behavioural change', *Psychological Review*, 84, 191–215.

References

Bangert-Drowns, R. L., Kulik, C. L. C., Kulik, J. A., and
    Morgan, M. T. (1991) 'The instructional effect of feedback in
    test-like events', *Review of Educational Research*, 61, 213–38.
Barnes, D. (1976) *From Curriculum to Communication*.
    Harmondsworth: Penguin.
Bauersfeld, H. (1988) 'Interaction, construction and
    knowledge: alternative perspectives for mathematics
    education', in D. Grouws, T. Cooney, and D. Jones (eds),
    *Effective Mathematics Teaching*. NCTM, Reston, VA:
    Lawrence Erlbaum, pp. 27–46.
Beaton, A., Mullis, I., Martin, M., Gonzales, E., Kelly, D., and
    Smith, T. (1996) *Mathematics Achievement in the Middle
    School Years: IEA's Third International Mathematics and
    Science Study*. Chestnut Hill, MA: Boston College.
Black, P. J. (1998a) *Testing: Friend or Foe? Theory and Practice of
    Assessment and Testing*. London: Falmer.
Black, P. J. (1998b) 'Formative assessment: raising standards
    inside the classroom', *School Science Review*, 80(291),
    39–46.
Black, P., Harrison, C., Lee, C., Marshall, B., and Wiliam, D.
    (2003) *Assessment for Learning: Putting it into Practice*.
    Maidenhead: Open University Press.
Black, P. J. and Wiliam, D. (1998a) 'Assessment and classroom
    learning', *Assessment in Education: Principles Policy and
    Practice*, 5(1), 7–73.
Black, P., and Wiliam, D. (1998b) *Inside the Black Box: Raising
    Standards through Classroom Assessment*. London: Kings
    College.
Blanchard, J. (1993) 'Keeping track: criterion based peer-
    assessment by pupils', *British Journal of Curriculum and
    Assessment*, 4(1), 37–42.
Brookhart, S. M. (2001) 'Successful students' formative and
    summative uses of assessment information', *Assessment in
    Education*, 8(2), 153–69.

Brookhart, S., Andolina, M., Zuza, M., and Furman, R. (2004) 'Minute Math: an action research study of student self-assessment', *Educational Studies in Mathematics*, 57, 213–27.

Brooks, V. (2002) *Assessment in Secondary Schools: The New Teacher's Guide to Monitoring, Assessment, Recording, Reporting and Accountability*. Buckingham: Open University Press.

Brophy, J. (1981) 'Teacher praise: a functional analysis', *Review of Educational Research*, 51(1), 5–32.

Brown, A. L. (1987) 'Metacognition, executive control, self regulation and other more mysterious mechanisms', in F. E. Weinert and R. H. Kluwe (eds), *Metacognition, Motivation and Understanding*. New Jersey: Lawrence Erlbaum, pp. 65–116.

Bruner, J. S. (1985) 'Vygotsky: a historical and conceptual perspective', in J. V. Wertsch (ed.), *Culture, Communication and Cognition: Vygotskian Perspectives*. Cambridge: CUP, pp. 21–34.

Bullock, K., and Wikeley, F. (2001) 'Personal learning planning: strategies for pupil learning', *Forum*, 43(2), 67–9.

Burns, C., and Myhill, D. (2004) 'Interactive or inactive? A consideration of the nature of interaction in whole class teaching', *Cambridge Journal of Education*, 34(1), 35–49.

Butler, R. (1987) 'Task-involving and ego-involving properties of evaluation: effects of different feedback conditions on motivational perceptions, interest and performance', *British Journal of Educational Psychology*, 79(4), 474–82.

Butler, R. (1988) 'Enhancing and undermining intrinsic motivation: the effects of task-involving and ego-involving evaluation on interest and performance', *British Journal of Educational Psychology*, 58, 1–14.

Cardelle-Elawar, M. (1992) 'Effects of teaching metacognitive skill to students with low mathematics ability', *Teaching and Teacher Education*, 8(2), 109–21.

# References

Cardelle-Elawar, M. (1995) 'Effects of metacognitive instruction on low achievers in mathematics problems', *Teaching and Teacher Education*, 11(1), 81–95.

Clarke, S. (1998) *Targeting Assessment in the Primary Classroom*. London: Hodder and Stoughton.

Clarke, S. (2005) *Formative Assessment in the Secondary Classroom*. London: Hodder Murray.

CLIO, (2000) *'Could try harder' – The LEARN Project: Guidance for Schools on Assessment for Learning*. Bristol: CLIO Centre for Assessment Studies.

Cobb, P., Boufi, A., McClain, K., and Whitenack, J. (1997) 'Reflective discourse and collective reflection', *Journal for Research in Mathematics Education*, 28(3), 258–77.

Daugherty, R. (1995) *National Curriculum Assessment: A Review of Policy 1987–1994*. London: The Falmer Press.

DfEE (Department for Education and Employment) (1997) *From Targets to Action*. London: DfEE.

DfEE (Department for Education and Employment) (1998) *The National Literacy Strategy: Framework for Teaching*. London: DfEE.

DfEE (Department for Education and Employment) (1999) *The National Numeracy Strategy: Framework for Teaching Mathematics*. Cambridge: Cambridge University Press.

DfEE, (Department for Education and Employment) (2001) *Key Stage 3 National Strategy: Framework for Teaching Mathematics: Years 7, 8 and 9*. London: DfEE.

DfES (Department for Education and Skills) (2005a) *Primary National Strategy*. http://www.standards. dfes.gov.uk/primary/ (accessed: 31.8.05).

DfES (Department for Education and Skills) (2005b) *The Key Stage Three National Strategy* http://www.standards.dfes.gov. uk/keystage3/downloads/ks3_3rdyearintro2km.pdf (accessed: 31.8.05).

Dweck, C.S. (1986) 'Motivational processes affecting learning', *American Psychologist (Special issue: psychological science and education)*, 41(10), 1040–8.

English, E., Hargreaves, L., and Hislam, J. (2002) 'Pedagogical dilemmas in the National Literacy Strategy', *Cambridge Journal of Education*, 32(1), 9–26.

Fernandes, M., and Fontana, D. (1996) 'Changes in control beliefs in Portuguese primary school pupils as a consequence of the employment of self-assessment strategies', *British Journal of Educational Psychology*, 66, 301–13.

Flavell, J. H. (1976) 'Metacognitive aspects of problem solving', in L. B. Resnick (ed.) *The Nature of Intelligence.* Hillsdale, NJ: Lawrence Erlbaum Associates, pp. 231–5.

Foos, P. W., Mora, J. J., and Tkacz, S. (1994) 'Student study techniques and the generation effect', *Journal of Educational Psychology*, 86(4), 567–76.

Foxman, D. (1985) *Mathematical Development: Review of the First Phase of Monitoring: Report on the Series of Annual Surveys of the Mathematical Performance of 11 and 15 Year Olds held from 1978–1982 Inclusive.* London: HMSO.

Freeman, R., and Lewis, R. (1998) *Planning and Implementing Assessment.* London: Kogan Page.

Fullan, M. (1991) *The New Meaning of Educational Change.* London: Cassell.

Gann, N. (1999) *Targets for Tomorrow's Schools: A Guide to Whole School Target Setting for Governors and Headteachers.* London: Falmer.

Gillborn, D., and Youdell, D. (2000) *Rationing Education.* Buckingham: Open University Press.

Gipps, C. (1994) *Beyond Testing: Towards a Theory of Educational Assessment.* London: Falmer.

Gipps, C. and Murphy, P. (1994) *A Fair Test? Assessment, Achievement and Equity.* Buckingham: Open University Press.

# References

Gipps, C., Brown, M., McCallum, B., and McAlister, S., (1995) *Intuition or evidence?* Buckingham: Open University Press.

Good, T. L., and Grouws, D. A., (1975) *Process-product Relationships in 4th Grade Mathematics Classrooms.* Report for National Institute of Education, Columbia, MO: University of Missouri (Report number: NE-G-00-0-0123).

Goodson, I. F., and Mangan, J. M. (1995) 'Subject cultures and the introduction of classroom computers', *British Journal of Educational Research*, 21(5), 613–28.

Gordon, S., and Rees, M., (1997) 'High stakes testing: worth the price?' *Journal of School Leadership*, 7, 345–68.

Graesser, A. C., Person, N. K., and Magliano, J. P. (1995) 'Collaborative dialogue patterns in naturalistic one-to-one tutoring', *Applied Cognitive Psychology*, 9, 495–522.

Hargreaves, D. (2004) *About Learning: Report of the Learning Working Group.* London: DEMOS.

Harlen, W., and Deakin Crick, R. (2002) 'A systematic review of the impact of summative assessment and tests on students' motivation for learning (EPPI-Centre review, version 1.1)', in *Research Evidence in Education Library*. London: EPPI-Centre, Social Science Research Unit, Institute of Education.

Harris, S., Nixon, J., and Ruddock, J. (1993) 'School work, homework and gender', *Gender and Education*, 5(1), 3–15.

Hart, K. (1981) *Children's Understanding of Mathematics: 11–16.* London: John Murray.

Holt, M. (1996) 'The making of Casablanca and the making of the curriculum', *Journal of Curriculum Studies*, 28(3), 241–52.

James, M. (1998) *Using Assessment for School Improvement.* Oxford: Heinemann.

Jones, S. (1992) *The Assessment of Mathematical Modelling.* Unpublished M.Ed. dissertation, University of Wales, Swansea.

Jones, S., and Tanner, H. (2002) 'Teachers' interpretations of effective whole class interactive teaching in secondary mathematics classrooms', *Educational Studies*, 28(3), 265–74.

Jones, S., Tanner, H., and Treadaway, M. (2000) 'Raising standards in mathematics through effective classroom practice', *Teaching Mathematics and its Applications*, 19(3), 125–34.

Kellaghan, T., Madaus, G., and Raczek, A. (1996) *The Use of External Examinations to Improve Student Motivation*. Washington DC: AERA.

King, A. (1992) 'Facilitating elaborated learning through guided student-generated questioning', *Educational Psychologist*, 21(1), 111–26.

Kluger, A. N., and DeNisi, A. (1996) 'The effects of feedback interventions on performance: a historical view, a meta-analysis and a preliminary feedback intervention theory', *Psychological Bulletin*, 119(2), 254–84.

Kohn, A. (2000) *The Case Against Standardised Testing*. Portsmouth, NH: Heinemann.

Kyriacou, C., and Goulding, M. (2004). 'A systematic review of the impact of the Daily Mathematics Lesson in enhancing pupil confidence and competence in early mathematics', in *Research Evidence in Education Library*. London: EPPI-Centre, Social Science Research Unit, Institute of Education.

Lee, D. and Gavine, D. (2003) 'Goal-setting and self-assessment in Year 7 students', *Educational Research*, 45(1), 49–59.

Mortimore, P., Sammons, P., Thomas, S., (1994) 'School effectiveness and value added measures', *Assessment in Education*, 1(3), 315–31.

Mroz, M., Smith, F., and Hardman, F. (2000) 'The discourse of the literacy hour', *Cambridge Journal of Education*, 30(3), 379–90.

# References

Murphy, R., (1997) 'Drawing outrageous conclusions from national assessment results: where will it all end?', *British Journal of Curriculum and Assessment*, (7)2, 32–4.

Newman, D., Griffin, P., and Cole, M. (1989) *The Construction Zone: Working for Cognitive Change in School*. Cambridge: Cambridge University Press.

Ofsted (1998) *Secondary Education 1993–1997: A Review of Secondary Schools in England*. London: The Stationery Office.

Ofsted (2003) *Annual Report of Her Majesty's Chief Inspector of Schools: Standards and Quality in Education 2001/02*. London: The Stationery Office.

Ofsted (2004). *The Key Stage 3 Strategy: Evaluation of the Third Year*. London: The Stationery Office.

Piaget, J. (1977) *The Grasp of Consciousness: Action and Concept in the Young Child*. London: Routledge and Kegan Paul.

QCA (2001a) *Assessment for Learning*. http://www.qca.org.uk/ca/5-14/afl/ (accessed at 1.6.03).

QCA (2001b) *Using Assessment to Raise Achievement in Mathematics*. http://www.qca.org.uk/ca/5-14/afl/afl_maths.pdf (accessed: 1.12.01).

QCA (2005) *School Based Assessment. Assessment for Learning: Research into Practice*. http://www.qca.org.uk/downloads/supporting_evidence.pdf (accessed at 31.8.05).

Roberts, J. (2004) *Does Exposing Pupils to a Variety of Learning Strategies and Providing them with Opportunities to Review their Work Help Pupils to Learn How to Learn?* Unpublished M.A. dissertation, University of Wales, Swansea.

Ross, M., Radnor, H., Mitchell, S., and Bierton, C. (1993) *Assessing Achievement in the Arts*. Buckingham: Open University Press.

Ryan, J., and Williams, J. (2000) *Mathematical Discussions with Children: Exploring Methods and Misconceptions as a Teaching Strategy*. Manchester: University of Manchester Publishers.

Sadler, D. R. (1989) 'Formative assessment and the design of instructional systems', *Instructional Science*, 18, 119–44.

Sadler, D. R. (1998) 'Formative assessment: revisiting the territory', *Assessment in Education*, 5(1), 77–84.

Saunders, L. (1999a) 'A brief history of educational "value added": how did we get to where we are?' *School Effectiveness and School Improvement*, 10(2), 233–56.

Saunders, L. (1999b) *'Value Added' Measurement of School Effectiveness: A Critical Review*. NFER: Slough.

Schön, D. (1990) *Educating the Reflective Practitioner*. Oxford: Jossey-Bass Publishers.

Shayer, M. and Adey, P. (2002) *Learning Intelligence*. Buckingham: Open University Press.

Smith, E., and Gorad, S. (2005) ' "They don't give us our marks": the role of formative feedback in student progress', *Assessment in Education: Principles, Policy and Practice*, 12(1), 7–20.

Smith, F., Hardman, F., Wall, K., and Mroz, M. (2004) 'Interactive whole class teaching in the National Literacy and Numeracy Strategies', *British Educational Research Journal*, 30(3), 395–411.

Snow, R. E. (1996) 'Self-regulation as meta-conation', *Learning and Individual Difference*, 8(3), 261–7.

Stacey, K. (2005) 'Travelling the road to expertise: a longitudinal study of learning', paper in *The Proceedings of the 29th Conference of the International Group for the Psychology of Mathematics Education (PME-29)*, Melbourne 1, 19–36.

Stigler, P. G., Takako, K., Knoll, S., and Serrano, A. (1999) *The TIMSS Videotape Classroom Study: Methods and Findings from an Exploratory Research Project on Eighth Grade Mathematics Instruction in Germany, Japan and the United States, NCES99-074*. Washington DC: US Government Printing Office.

Swan, M. (1983) *Teaching Decimal Place Value: A Competitive Study of 'Conflict' and 'Positive Only' Approaches*. Nottingham: Shell Centre for Mathematical Education.

Sylva, K. (1994) 'School influences on children's development', *Journal of Child Psychology and Psychiatry*, 35(1), 135–70.

Tanner, H. (1992) 'Teacher assessment of mathematics in the National Curriculum at Key Stage 3', *Welsh Journal of Education*, 3(2), 27–34.

Tanner, H. (1997) *Using and Applying Mathematics: Developing Mathematical Thinking through Practical Problem Solving and Modelling*. Unpublished Ph.D Thesis, University of Wales, Swansea.

Tanner, H., and Jones, S. (1994) 'Using peer and self-assessment to develop modelling skills with students aged 11 to 16: a socio-constructive view', *Educational Studies in Mathematics*, 27(4), 413–31.

Tanner, H., and Jones, S. (1995) 'Teaching mathematical thinking skills to accelerate cognitive development', in *The Proceedings of Psychology of Mathematics Education Conference (PME-19)*, Recife, Brazil, (3), 121–8.

Tanner, H. and Jones, S. (1999) 'Dynamic scaffolding and reflective discourse: the impact of teaching style on the development of mathematical thinking', in *The Proceedings of the 23rd Conference of the International Group for the Psychology of Mathematics Education (PME23)*, Haifa, (4), 257–64.

Tanner, H., and Jones, S. (2000a) 'Scaffolding for success: reflective discourse and the effective teaching of mathematical thinking skills', in T. Rowland and C. Morgan (eds), *Research in Mathematics Education Volume 2: Papers of the British Society for Research into Learning Mathematics*. London: British Society for Research into Learning Mathematics, pp. 19–32.

Tanner, H., and Jones, S. (2000b) *Becoming a Successful Teacher of Mathematics*. London: Routledge/Falmer.

Tanner, H., and Jones, S. (2003a) 'Assessing children's mathematical thinking in practical modelling situations', *Teaching Mathematics and its Applications*, 21(4), 145–59.

Tanner, H., and Jones, S. (2003b) 'Self-efficacy in mathematics and students' use of self-regulated learning strategies during assessment events', in *The Proceedings of the 27th Conference of the International Group for the Psychology of Mathematics Education (PME27)*, Hawaii, (4), 275–8.

Tanner, H., and Jones, S. (2003c) *Marking and Assessment*. London: Continuum.

Tanner, H., Jones, S., and Davies, A. (2002) *Developing Numeracy in the Secondary School*. London: David Fulton Publishers.

Tanner, H., Jones, S., and Treadaway, M. (1999) 'Schools that add value: raising standards in mathematics', in *The Proceedings of the British Educational Research Association (BERA-99), Brighton*. http://www.leeds.ac.uk/educol/bera99.htm (accessed 6.9.04).

Tanner, H., Jones, S., Kennewell, S., and Beauchamp, G. (2005) 'Interactive whole class teaching and interactive white boards', in *The Proceedings of The Mathematics Education Research Group of Australasia (MERGA28)*, Melbourne.

Torrance, H., and Prior, J. (1998) *Investigating Formative Assessment: Teaching, Learning and Assessment in the Classroom*. Buckingham: Open University Press.

Von Glasersfeld, E. (ed.) (1991) *Radical Constructivism in Mathematics Education*. Dordrecht: Kluwer.

Vygotsky, L. S. (1978) in M. Cole, V. John-Steiner, S. Scribner, and E. Souberman (eds), *Mind in Society: The Development of Higher Psychological Processes*. Cambridge, Mass.: Harvard University Press.

Weeden, P., Winter, J., and Broadfoot, P. (2002) *Assessment: What's In It for Schools?* London: Routledge/Falmer.

# References

Wiliam, D. (1992) 'Some technical issues in assessment: a user's guide', *British Journal of Curriculum and Assessment*, 2(3), 11–20.

Wiliam, D. (1999a) 'Formative assessment in Mathematics: Part 1: rich questioning', *Equals*, Summer, 5(2), 15–18.

Wiliam, D. (1999b) 'Formative assessment in Mathematics: Part 2: feedback', *Equals*, Autumn, 5(3), 8–13.

Wiliam, D. (2000) 'Formative assessment in Mathematics: Part 3: the learner's role', *Equals*, Summer, 6(1), 18–22.

Wolters, C. A. and Rosenthal, H. (2000) 'The relation between students' motivational beliefs and their use of motivational regulation strategies', *International Journal of Educational Research*, 33(7–8), 801–20.

Wood, T. (1994) 'Patterns of interaction and the culture of mathematics classrooms', in S. Lerman (ed.), *Cultural Perspectives on the Mathematics Classroom*, pp. 149–68. Dordrecht, Netherlands: Kluwer Academic Publishers.

Wood, D., and Wood, H. (1996) 'Contingency in teaching and learning', *Learning and Instruction*, 6(4), 391–7.

Wragg, E. C. (2005) *The Art and Science of Teaching and Learning: The Collected Works of Ted Wragg*. London: Routledge Falmer.